PRISONERS of WAR in
BEDFORDSHIRE

PRISONERS of WAR in BEDFORDSHIRE

STEPHEN RISBY

AMBERLEY

First published 2011

Amberley Publishing
Cirencester Road, Chalford,
Stroud, Gloucestershire, GL6 8PE

www.amberleybooks.com

Copyright © Stephen Risby 2011

The right of Stephen Risby to be identified as the Author
of this work has been asserted in accordance with the
Copyrights, Designs and Patents Act 1988.

British Library Cataloguing in Publication Data.
A catalogue record for this book is available from the British Library.

ISBN 978-1-4456-0312-4

Typesetting and Origination by Amberley Publishing.
Printed in Great Britain.

Contents

Introduction

In 2007, I undertook a course at Madingley College, Cambridge. Aiming for an Advanced Diploma in Local History, I commenced to study prisoners of war in the Second World War. Too large a subject to examine in detail on a national basis, I focused it in the context of north Bedfordshire, and specifically, where possible, the PoW camp at Bolnhurst (also known as Ducks Cross or Colmworth). I produced a paper, the purpose of which was to re-examine the reality of Italian PoW life and establish if it matched present-day perception and memory. The amount of research material exceeded what I could use at Madingley. To make it available to a wider audience, I have produced this enlarged and detailed work, now including additional comment upon German PoW.

Hopefully this book has explained the importance of labour requirements, which led to first Italian and then German PoW being brought to Great Britain. While using examples from north Bedfordshire to demonstrate how PoW lived and worked, I hope readers from further afield will recognise that the attitudes of both public and prisoners, and their wartime environment, was paralleled across this country.

I have looked briefly at the history of relations between Great Britain, Italy and Germany in an attempt to identify how preconceptions of the Italian and German were formed. I explain how and why, in my opinion, the interaction between the public and PoW failed to meet these expectations. On the whole, the British people came to realise that there was little difference between themselves and these groups, but sometimes there was conflict. As an illustration of this I have included details of the murder of a British soldier in Tilbrook, and the subsequent death of his PoW killer.

Geoffrey Field once wrote: 'In an effort to break through the impeding layers of nostalgia and demythologise the war years, historians have paid growing attention to aspects of life omitted from the 'orthodox' heroic versions, such as looting, black market activities, absenteeism, strikes, cynicism, and low morale.'[1] I hope this book will assist this process.

This publication cannot be considered the definitive work on the subject. I am sure there is more evidence yet to be found, and stories to record.

ABBREVIATIONS

BLARS	Bedfordshire and Luton Archive and Records Service
Coy	Company
DP	Displaced Persons
EVW	European Voluntary Worker
GPOWWC	German Prisoner of War Working Camp
HMSO	His (Her) Majesty's Stationary Office
ICRC	International Committee of the Red Cross
IWC	Italian Working Company
NFU	National Farmers' Union
TNA	The National Archive
PoW	Prisoner(s) of War
POWE	Political Warfare Executive
REME	Royal Electrical & Mechanical Engineers
WLA	Women's Land Army

Acknowledgements

In researching this book I would like to thank the following for their help: John Shelton for permitting me to dredge up unwelcome memories; Eddi Petri and Hans Pueschel for explaining PoW life at Ducks Cross from a German perspective; Carol Lack and Jon Mills for photographs; John Sainsbury for translation of documents; Stephen Coleman, Historic Environment Information Officer for Bedfordshire County Council; and the staff at Bedfordshire and Luton Archive and Records Service, Huntingdon Record Office, The National Archives and British Museum Newspaper Library, together with everyone else who assisted me.

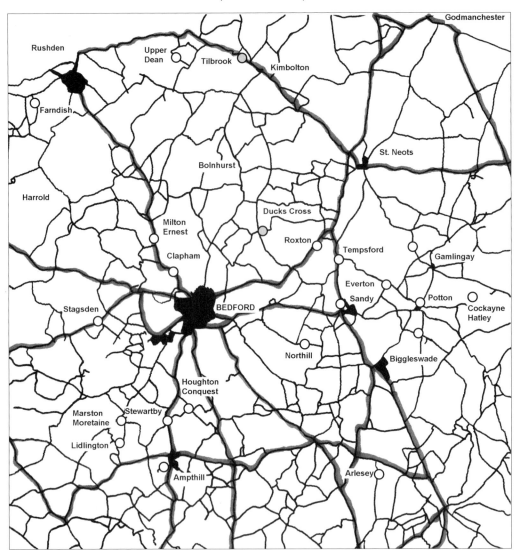

A map of Bedford and the surrounding area, showing the primary locations of PoW camps. (Not to scale.)

CHAPTER I

Historical Background

The Second World War was the last example of 'total war' in Britain. All the resources of the British Empire and its people were utilised to ensure final victory. The competing demands for resources nationally necessitated extraordinary responses. One of the resources that became available to the British government was prisoner of war (PoW) labour. This chapter will briefly outline why PoW from the Axis powers came to be in Britain.

Following the declaration of war in 1939, the demand for manpower from the armed services required the mobilisation of the Territorial Army and conscription was soon introduced. In September 1939, 247 Territorial Army men had been mobilised in 5th Battalion, Bedfordshire and Hertfordshire Regiment, alone. Figures for its duplicate, 6th Battalion, and the Bedfordshire Yeomanry, Royal Engineers and other Territorial Army units are unknown, but together they probably exceeded 1,000 men. In total, 12,000 men were conscripted from Luton during the war.

The resulting reduction in the available male workforce had an adverse effect upon agricultural production nationwide. A. W. Gale wrote to the *Farmers Weekly*, 'If our trained men are taken, and farmers have to replace them with land girls and "conchies" [conscientious objectors] it is impossible to secure the maximum output from the land.'[2] By the beginning of 1942, it is estimated that, nationally, 83,000 men had left agriculture for the armed services.[3] At the same time, the German U-boat blockade and the loss of European sources led to shortages of many goods, especially foodstuffs.

The shortfall in food imports had to be made good by increased domestic food production. To achieve this more workers were required and derelict farmland had to be brought back into cultivation. As a result of low market prices for cereal crops between the wars, nationally farmers turned to dairy farming, resulting in neglect of drains, ditches and fences. Large tracts of arable farmland became derelict.[4] In 1941, across Great Britain, about 40,000 farm drainage schemes were approved, covering 1,214,000 acres. A further 1,900,000 schemes were covered between 1942 and 1944. It is impossible to determine what percentages of these were in Bedfordshire, but the Ouse Conservancy Board undertook much work.

There were many proposed solutions to the agricultural worker shortage, all of them being attempts to make better use of existing resources. One was to use 'directed men', such as the aforementioned conscientious objectors, and the unemployed, who could be compelled by law to take such employment as was found for them. Despite the existence of statutory authority there was reluctance by the Ministry of Labour to direct men into lower-paid industries, such as farming.

Another suggestion, to form Agricultural Companies in the Pioneer Corps was rejected, although the Ministry of Agriculture borrowed some 3,000 soldiers for land reclamation work. However, with the threat of invasion still looming, all soldiers were primarily needed for defence work, so this was not a long-term option.

One additional source of labour was the Women's Land Army (WLA), which by August 1941 was over 19,000 strong.[5] These measures all proved inadequate for the task. In November 1941, the Food Policy Committee warned that 'if the men now liable for military service were taken out of the industry it was doubtful whether home production would reach the 1941 figure and it was most improbable that it would reach the present objective for 1942'.[6] Another option was needed.

The total number PoW in Britain during March 1940 was only 257.[7] By 8 June 1941 that number had risen, but did not exceed 3,800.[8] By December 1940, the Allied victories in the 'Western Desert' had resulted in the taking of 35,940 Italian PoW. These were a burdensome result of victory that required feeding and guarding, but provided nothing useful in return. It was later suggested that Italian PoW be brought from the Middle East to Britain to provide the required labour force.

An inter-departmental government meeting was held on 12 February 1941 to determine the numbers of Italian prisoners of war who could be employed in the United Kingdom. Submissions from the departments concerned showed that in the first instance 9,775 could be employed. Those attending felt that the following advantages would accrue from the employment of Italian PoW: relief of the acute labour shortage in certain areas, particularly in the building and construction of camps; a supply of skilled labour for repairs to mechanical transport; assistance in farm work and food production; and important work in forestry and land reclamation. Considering the manpower shortages, the estimated number of PoW required seems under-ambitious.[9]

Captured Italians during the North African conflict, 1942. Many of these men would be employed to work in Britain during their captivity.

The representatives stated: 'It is the intention to select carefully only such prisoners who are skilled in the work upon which they will be employed, and great care will be exercised that only non-violent types are brought into this scheme.'[10] The PoW selected had to be white Italians, not soldiers from Italian colonies or officers.[11] No reason was given for this prejudice. Soldiers from the agricultural south were preferred to those from the more educated and industrialised north of Italy. Attempts were made to exclude fascist, air force and naval prisoners, presumably as they were those considered most likely to be politically disruptive or have skills to enable them to escape.[12]

Italian PoW were predominantly 'other ranks', but some officers were brought to the UK, mainly medical doctors and Catholic priests, to administer to the prisoners' needs in camp. It was contrary to the Geneva Convention for officers to be required to undertake work so they were considered unnecessary mouths to feed. Their leadership was also potentially disruptive in British eyes.

On 26 March 1941, Bedfordshire was only one of twelve counties responding to a government suggestion concerning use of Italian PoW labour. Bedfordshire War Agricultural Committee replied that it could use up to 500 men in any part of the county not in a prohibited area. By 'prohibited area' it meant the south of the county, which contained sensitive military installations, and was already subject to restrictions regarding 'Alien' access.

The next hurdle to be overcome was how to transport the PoW to this country. Shipping was in short supply, but space was made available in boats returning un-laden from the Middle East. A slow dribble of Italians began to arrive; numbers were limited, not only due to the lack of available transportation to Britain, but also the availability of guards and accommodation. Living space was maximised by transferring German PoW to Canada and constructing new camps. The government would have liked to use more than were available.

From early 1941, batches of PoW were employed on drainage and reclamation schemes under the County War Agricultural Executive Committees. They were described after arrival as 'some very good material of good physique and with a willingness to work. Whilst there were a small number of agriculturists among them, few had any experience with tractors and most had worked exclusively with oxen and ploughs. The remainder were of peasant stock, adept with sickle, scythe and spade who would be ideal for ditching and draining work.'[13]

On 14 August 1942, Italian PoW imprisoned in Empire countries were thus: South Africa – 59,750; East Africa (Kenya) – 57,608; Middle East – 25,317; India – 67,525.[14] By the end of 1943, nearly 50,000 Italian PoW were employed in agriculture in Britain. In January 1942, there were about sixty PoW camps in Great Britain. The first Italian PoW were imprisoned in existing Ministry of Agriculture hostels until camps were constructed. Camp numbers swelled considerably during the next two years. By 14 April 1945, this number had increased to over 200 camps and hospitals, and 102 Working Companies, the latter administered by twenty-seven Pioneer Groups.

The PoW labour scheme was based on that implemented during the Great War.[15] Initially, working gangs were taken out of camp under army escort. Soon after their arrival, it became obvious that the government thought Italian PoW were living up to preconceived expectation. The policy was therefore amended on 2 January 1942, when the Ministry of Agriculture and Fisheries announced that Italian PoW were to use ten hostels experimentally. This included one at Leighton Buzzard as a satellite of Aylesbury PoW Camp. Under the trial scheme, PoW would live under guard in hostels at night, but would be released to a farmer's custody each day.

Prior to the introduction of hostels, the army expressed concern in November 1941: 'As the War Office feel that complaints are likely to be made by the public they request that the scheme should be forwarded to the Lord President by the [Security] Executive and that he should be asked to give an assurance on behalf of the Cabinet that the Secretary of State for War will not be responsible either to the Cabinet or to

Parliament for escapes or misbehaviour on the part of prisoners arising through the scheme.'[16]

The fears about Italians escaping were ill-founded. Responding to a War Office letter, dated 15 January 1942, Eastern Command stated that 'no special difficulty has been encountered in opening any of the Italian PoW Hostels, but that none have been open long enough to form a final opinion. At present the scheme seems to be working smoothly.'[17] There were subsequent escapes and absences nationally, but not on a large scale, and none are known to have made a 'home run' from this island. These escapes continued through to the end of the war, a subject that will be returned to.

The success of the agricultural policy led to further use of the newly found labour pool. On 6 October 1942, consideration was requested of a proposal for employing 1,700 PoW in Eastern Command in eight specific categories including Royal Engineer dumps, Royal Engineer stores, and Command supply depots. The reasoning behind the request was the serious labour shortages resulting from the withdrawal of army Pioneer Companies; the availability of the PoW during the non-agricultural season; and the lack of security needed for their employment, which should not present undue difficulty. It was not considered that their proposed employment would directly infringe the Geneva Convention, so long as the prisoners were engaged directly on war work. This proposal appears to have been pre-empted by a letter to the War Office dated 17 September 1942. It stated that the Deputy Director of Mechanical Engineering at Eastern Command wished to employ thirty Italian prisoners of war for dismantling motorcycles at a Workshop Vehicle Park that was acutely short of labour. On 21 September 1942, the War Office approved the allotment of these PoW for work at REME Workshops, Buntingford, Hertfordshire.[18]

It appears to be a direct consequence of this decision that Italian, and later German, PoW were subsequently employed in non-agricultural war work. With the later acceptance of Italians as co-operators, these units subsequently became Working Companies of the Pioneer Corps in their own right. Post-war, the concerns about complying with the Geneva Convention dissipated as German PoW were engaged upon bomb-disposal and mine-clearance duties.

When it became apparent that the hostel scheme was working, another scheme was introduced where prisoners were billeted out.[19] They lived either in farm buildings or other unoccupied local housing and both farmer and PoW were subject to restrictions. These were laid out in Ministry of Agriculture and Fisheries forms P.W.1, P.W.2, and P.W.3 (see Appendix 1). Farmers voluntarily accepted these PoW labourers, who were housed locally, without guards.

On 13 August 1943, the Home Office recorded that local police would vet farmers, with whom it was proposed to billet PoW, as 'cases have arisen of prisoners being billeted on farmers whose loyalty was suspected, or who were otherwise undesirable'. It is unknown how many, if any, were vetted by Bedfordshire Police.

Allied troops had landed in Sicily on 9 July 1943. On 5 August, the Italian government signed an armistice, formally surrendering three days later. This resulted in the Germans, who occupied northern Italy, taking 450,000 Italian prisoners. Control of large numbers of Allied PoW passed from Italian to German captivity. Negotiations to exchange Allied prisoners in Italian hands for Italians under Allied control failed. Italy neither had the Allied prisoners to exchange, nor was there a willingness by Britain to release Italians while there was only an armistice, and not a peace treaty, in place. The Allies were split as to how to treat Italian PoW. In North Africa, the Geneva Convention was no longer considered applicable, and Italians undertook war work. General Eisenhower, commander of Allied Forces in the Mediterranean, paroled Italians in Italy after their army engaged in hostilities against Germany.

In Britain, the desperate need for agricultural labour remained. However, in order to retain the vital workforce, Italian PoW were to be given the opportunity to elect to become 'co-operators'. The range of co-operators' employment opportunities was widened to include war work, and the conditions of their imprisonment, including uniforms, was relaxed.

On Sunday 30 April 1944, all Italian PoW in camps were paraded and informed of new arrangements for co-operation. Volunteers were to be organised into Italian Labour Battalions. Less than 60 per cent of Italian PoW volunteered.[20] The remainder were returned to camps and treated as PoW. Sadly Britain subsequently reneged on some of the promised improved conditions. Subsequently, it was Italian Fascists, who had failed to co-operate and had become a burden, who were repatriated first, giving rise to some disillusionment among co-operators remaining in Britain.

Following the invasion of the European mainland in June 1944, large numbers of German prisoners were taken. Between 1940 and late 1944, it had been official government policy not to retain Germans who held Nazi sympathies in Britain. This was on the grounds of national security and fears of them escaping during any German invasion attempt. Such prisoners were initially sent to Canada, and later to the USA as well. To provide an insight into the problems, in March 1944 only 55,235 German PoW were held by the western Allies. By December 1944, the number had risen to 270,561.

The number of Germans taken prisoner at the end of the war has led to subsequent allegations of their deliberate neglect by the Americans while still in Europe. In March 1945, General Eisenhower, by now Supreme Allied Commander in Western Europe, had obtained agreement to treat the surrendered German armies not as PoW, but as Disarmed Enemy Forces, denying them the protection of the Geneva Convention. It has been claimed that, by 1946, a total of 793,239 died while in makeshift camps, and although the numbers have been challenged, there is no doubt that abuse did take place.[21]

While the initial plan to deal with these PoW had been to divide them equally among the western Allies, during the winter of 1945, 175,000 German PoW were taken to the USA and 'held on account of the UK as British prisoners'. Britain was unable to look after them. Eventually the holding of German PoW in Britain was forced upon the British government. This was because there was neither the capability to hold them properly in the liberated areas of Europe, nor the continued political will or available shipping to transport them across the Atlantic. In 1946, men held 'on account' in America were not repatriated to Germany but returned to Britain. This caused ill feeling among the Germans already in Britain, especially when the USA released hardened Nazis from their quota ahead of pro-democratic prisoners held in Britain.

The need was also recognised for a long-term substitute for the Italians post-war. The holding of German PoW in Britain resulted in accommodation shortages, reducing the potential numbers of Italians who might otherwise have been utilised in this country. From the agricultural labour perspective this was a disadvantage.

Initially, German PoW sat idle in their camps. Boredom was recognised as likely to ferment resentment and trouble, therefore agreement was reluctantly given to their employment. Like the early Italians, the Germans were only permitted to work in gangs under an armed escort and consequently the range of jobs they could be given to do was much restricted. Employment was supposedly not an option for SS soldiers or Luftwaffe personnel, but in due course this rule lapsed.

In the autumn of 1944, however, when there were fears that the harvest might not be gathered in full, nor the potatoes lifted because of the persistent bad weather, and the Allied Forces could offer farmers only reduced help, an experiment was performed. Small groups of Germans were allowed to work unescorted in the fields. This proved successful, leading to liberalised German PoW conditions. Eventually, German PoW would live in hostels and be billeted with farmers in much the same manner as the Italians before them.

By the end of the European War, there were about 224,000 prisoners of war in Britain (131,800 were Italians, the remainder German and their allies[22]), of which 130,000 were employed in agriculture.[23] This is out of a total of 381,632 German and 153,779 Italians who were then in Allied custody.[24] By early 1948, all Italians had been repatriated.

Within Bedfordshire it appears to have become accepted history that the Italian community in Bedford originated from the PoW who remained after the end of the war. This is misleading, as the local Italian community started with a recruitment drive in Italy by the London Brick Company in the late 1940s, as part of the European Volunteer Worker Scheme. A few of the migrant workers were ex-Italian PoW and some had obtained work visas and returned to work on the farms around the county.[25] The national policy to forcibly provide a foreign labour force during wartime conditions has, therefore, left its mark upon post-war society.

CHAPTER 2

Local Detail

Having reviewed why the British government found it necessary to utilise PoW to support the survival of the nation, this chapter will endeavour to paint the local picture around Bedfordshire.

A proposal to build the county's first 'working camp' at Bolnhurst was made on 2 January 1942. War Office records show that there was already a PoW camp, numbered 72, based at the Ministry of Agriculture Hostel at Bolnhurst. By 9 February, construction was planned and under consideration. On 14 March 1942, approval was given to open the Bolnhurst facility, titled 72 Prisoner of War Camp (PoW Camp), officially addressed at Ducks Cross, Wilden. Army Pioneers, building the new camp, were lodged at the nearby Bolnhurst Ministry of Agriculture Hostel. No contemporary plan of the camp survives and it is impossible to interpret the use to which huts remaining on site today were put. However, a map survives of an unidentified camp in the locality of Holford Road that gives us a clue as to how Ducks Cross may have been utilised, even if the layout was different.

Prior to Ducks Cross Camp opening, the nearest 'working' camps had been No. 26 Barton Field Camp, Ely; No. 29 Royston Heath Camp; and No. 36 Hartwell Dog Track Camp, Aylesbury.

The new camp eventually comprised of about forty-three permanent huts, mainly constructed of wood, for the prisoners. These were surrounded by a wire fence, which probably only provided a notional defence against escape. Outside of the prisoners' compound was another group of between twenty-seven and thirty huts. These provided the accommodation for British staff and various administration and medical facilities. A sewage plant was built for the camp enabling the ablution blocks to have efficient sanitation. Electricity was also provided.

The Italians' Roman Catholic religious beliefs were maintained and encouraged during imprisonment. A chapel was somewhere that the

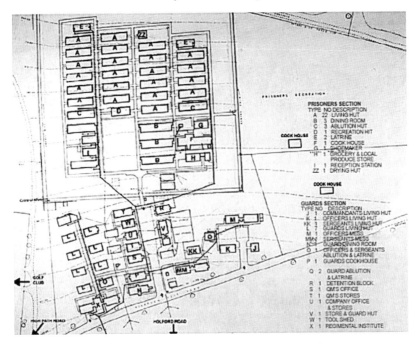

A plan of the Holford Road PoW camp.

An aerial view of Ducks Cross taken in 1945 provides a general overview of the camp layout.

The camp's post-war existence in the 1960s.

Italian PoW could express them. At Ducks Cross they converted a hut into a chapel, painting murals onto the walls. Sadly, today only photographs of their work have survived.

The policy of housing PoW in guarded camps was amended on 22 December 1941. On 2 January 1942, the Ministry of Agriculture and Fisheries announced that Italian PoW were to use ten hostels experimentally. This included a satellite of Aylesbury PoW Camp at Leighton Buzzard.

The Leighton Buzzard hostel was to be occupied by fifty PoW on 27 January 1942, but it did not remain open long. A memorandum dated 12 February 1942 recorded that the Air Ministry considered Italian PoW engaged in agricultural work near a very secret RAF Signals establishment undesirable, despite prior approval having been given by the Security Executive. Apparently the Air Ministry's consent had been previously granted because they did not:

The PoW chapel altar.

A mural in the Italian PoW chapel depicting the Crucifixion.

a) want to spoil the experiment by refusing to allow any hostels to be put up within ten miles of an aerodrome.

b) think that the Leighton Buzzard hostel would be as near as it is to a highly secret signals establishment, nor within an Aliens Protected Area (No. 4).

According to Group Captain Plant on 17 February, 'People in the neighbourhood know that the aliens have been cleared out and are, therefore, alarmed at the sight of the prisoners, that, more than this, the local Police and the officer commanding the station are anxious that they should go.' The support of both the Admiralty and Air Commodore Blackford was behind the relocation of these PoW.

The Home Office had also heard of the case from the local chief constable, who was strongly of the opinion that the men should be removed. This statement was slightly at odds with an official memorandum on the following day. Reporting on the fifty PoW at Leighton Buzzard, it said that 'of these, 13 work for individual farmers and 32 in gangs'. All have been fully employed and had done satisfactory work. Local public opinion had been favourable. The same day H. J. Johns, Ministry of Agriculture and Fisheries, recorded that the Italians would be relocated. He proposed moving the PoW back to their original camp. The prisoners left Leighton Buzzard at 2 p.m. on 19 February and were transferred not to Aylesbury but to the Ministry of Agriculture hostel at Ampthill.

When considering the proximity of Ducks Cross to the airfields at Thurleigh, Twinwood Farm and Tempsford, it is surprising that 72 PoW Camp was built there at all.

No complete list of PoW hostels and camps in Bedfordshire has been found yet. From information available, it is only possible to compile brief accounts of those so far located.

HQ 9 Group, Pioneer Corps: On 14 April 1945 it was located at 8 Rothsay Gardens, Bedford. Under command were 561 Italian Working Coy (IWC), 576 IWC, 583 IWC, 607 IWC, 611 IWC, 628 IWC and 644 IWC.

On 11 November 1945, still commanding these units, HQ 9 Group had by now relocated from Bedford to 22 Priory Road, Dunstable.

Ampthill: The Ampthill hostel flourished after the transfer of PoW from Leighton Buzzard to the Ministry of Agriculture hostel known as Park Road on 19 January 1942. It remained in use until shortly before the last PoW were repatriated.

On 2 March 1942, the County War Agricultural Executive Committee mentioned the hostel having forty-five prisoners working in parties of

Italian chapel art depicting the Nativity.

Italian chapel art portraying the Resurrection.

two, three or four for individual farmers. No prisoners worked in gangs. All had been fully employed and had done satisfactory work. There was a waiting list of local farmers wanting to use PoW labour. There were no reports of fraternisation, but there was a certain amount of public comment due to the fact that prisoners lived in excellent conditions compared with soldiers, and guards received only half the cigarette ration of their prisoners. By 18 August 1942, the hostel had been temporarily utilised for other civilian labour as the sixteen PoW based here were now all billeted on farms. While all the PoW had been fully utilised there had been two cases where the military had to take unspecified action in respect of the PoW residents. There had also been one case of fraternisation, which was dealt with.[26]

On September 1945, this hostel was still used as a 72 PoW Camp satellite hostel and contained Italian PoW residents.

In November 1945, Ampthill hostel was utilising the ex-Women's Land Army camp in Houghton Road. This location is difficult to identify today as no road leads directly from Ampthill to Houghton Conquest. There is a derelict Houghton House just north of Ampthill, to which an unnamed lane runs from the town. Photos also survive of another camp, to the south of Park Road, opposite 614 PoW Camp, which has been referred to as a hostel. Ampthill, therefore, had both a hostel and a camp existing simultaneously. The existence of an unidentified Italian PoW hostel in the vicinity of Houghton Conquest and its proximity to Ampthill raise the possibility that both hostels were using an identical location, with differing designations.

By 12 January 1943, satellite hostels for 72 PoW Camp had been proposed at Woburn Road, Ampthill.

After 14 April 1945, there is mention made of 261 GPOWWC, War Department Camp, Ampthill. This was not based in the existing hostel. Air reconnaissance photos taken on 13 June 1947 show buildings to the north side of Park Road, then known as Woburn Road, which are believed to be this camp. German PoW from here worked in Wrest Park cultivating vegetables. This camp was demolished in February 1949; the land became today's football pitches.

On 13 August 1943, it was reported by the IRCC that a hostel for 614 German PoW was operating in Ampthill. It is believed it was on the opposite side of Park Road to 261 GPOWWC. This camp was also demolished and the Cheshire Home now stands on its site.

Arlesey: In September 1943, 29 PoW Camp at Royston, Hertfordshire, had a hostel at the Command supply depot in Arlesey, Bedfordshire. The location of the hostel was adjacent to that of the Eastern Command supply depot, which in 1941 had been at the Portland Cement Works in Arlesey.

Bedford: During September 1943, Italian PoW were attached to Pioneer Corps Companies at Bedford, reporting to the War Department.[27]

In November 1945, Bedford hostel is listed, with a map reference that located it in brickworks off the A418 near Kempston Hardwick, some four miles south of Bedford. The hostel was possibly identical to a Women's Land Army hostel at Chimney Corner that had also been used as an Italian, and later a German, hostel. The PoW here were attached to a nearby Pioneer Corps Company.

Biggleswade: On 30 December 1943, there was a proposal submitted to build a new hostel in Biggleswade.

Clapham: Also in existence in April 1945 was 278 PoW Camp at Green Lane, Clapham, which supplied German PoW working parties to Lidlington and Ridgemont brickworks. Photographs taken at Clapham on 23 August 1946 show this to be a tented camp with a few huts, presumably for messing and administration purposes. There were attempts at improvements to the camp made by the German PoW, who were reported to have stolen bricks from their employer to make the paths seen in the picture.[28] A chicken farm behind The Woodlands Hotel is believed to have occupied the site post-war. Today the site is used for caravan storage and a nursery school.

Cockayne Hatley: The camp was located in about twenty Nissen type huts in 3 acres to the back of The Old Rectory, Village Road. One concrete base remains. The Old Rectory itself was the camp mess. Cockayne Hatley Hall was possibly used as the British camp staff quarters. Initially, the camp was for Germans and was wired and guarded. Once the Italians moved in, security was relaxed.

By 1946/47, it was occupied by Germans, as a satellite of Potton camp.

Ducks Cross: 72 PoW Camp, Bolnhurst.

Everton: A WRAF hostel, complete with red carpet tiles, was located opposite playing fields in Everton. Sometime between 1946 and 1947, after WRAF had vacated this camp, the WO, fearing squatters, moved German PoW from Potton Camp into the hut. This area has since been built on.

Gamlingay: On 14 April 1945, No. 561 IWC was located in the grounds of Old Woodbury Hall, Gamlingay, Sandy, Beds.

The tented camp at Clapham. (*BLARS Z50 29 13 & BLARS Z50 29 14*)

By 2 November 1945, this camp had been taken over by 269 German Prisoner Working Company. It became a satellite of Potton camp, housing German PoW.

Godmanchester: By 12 January 1943, a satellite hostel for 72 PoW Camp had been proposed at Godmanchester, St Ives District, Huntingdonshire. Details are unknown.

Harrold: On 14 April 1945, No. 611 IWC was based in the grounds of Harrold Hall, Harrold. This hall has now been demolished and a new housing estate built in the grounds.

Highlands Farm: By 12 January 1943, satellite hostels for 72 PoW Camp had been proposed at Highlands Farm, Bedford Road, Northill (which was also referred to as Moggerhanger Hostel, Northill District).

In September 1943, hostels at Highlands Farm supplied labour for the Ministry of Agriculture.

On September 1945, this hostel was still used as a 72 PoW Camp satellite hostel and contained Italian PoW residents.

Houghton Conquest: On 12 June 1943, mention is made of fifty-five Italian PoW from 72 PoW Camp having been accommodated with 221 Pioneer Coy at Houghton Conquest from then until the end of month.

Lidlington: In September 1943, hostels in Lidlington and Bedford both reported to the War Department.[29]

In November 1945, a hostel is listed attached to a Pioneer Corps Company at the Command supply depot at Lidlington Station. Map references for the hostel placed CSD Lidlington Station less than half a mile from Church Farm, Marston Mortaine. These two hostels may be identical.

Marston Mortaine: On 14 April 1945, No. 576 IWC was based at Church Farm, Marston Mortaine, Bedfordshire. The first mention of PoW at this location was on 28 May 1943. Orders were received by 297 Company, Pioneer Corps, to prepare to receive fifty Italian PoW, who would assist them at 11 Main Supply Depot, Marston Mortaine. To comply with the Geneva Convention the British soldiers were made to sleep under canvas and the Italians were given their huts! To add insult to injury, nineteen days later, on 16 June, the Pioneer Corps were told to surrender their premises at 3, 15, 16, 17 and 28 Jubilee Cottages, Marston Mortaine, to the ladies of the Auxiliary Territorial Service.

Milton Ernest: In September 1945, five of 72 PoW Camp's satellite hostels contained Italian PoW residents, including one at Milton Ernest.

Peterborough: On 5 March 1946, 702 PoW Camp at Kingscliff, Peterborough, was reorganised as 702 Base Transit Camp, No. 1 German PoW Holding Unit. It acted as the reception centre for all PoW held by the RAF in this country. This camp supplied resident working parties to RAF stations located throughout East Anglia. In the last quarter of 1946, Luftwaffe PoW from this camp were detached to the following locations in Bedfordshire: 13 Maintenance Unit at RAF Henlow; RAF Milton Ernest; RAF Wing, near Leighton Buzzard; RAF Leighton Buzzard and RAF Cranfield. Considering the fuss made about the first hostel at Leighton Buzzard, this was a considerable 'about turn' by the RAF.

Potton: On 14 April 1945, No. 628 IWC operated from Hutted Camp, Sutton Park, Potton, Bedfordshire. These huts were located adjacent to Biggleswade Road on what is now the John O'Gaunt Golf Club course. Subsequently, 269 German PoW Working Camp replaced 628 IWC. The address for 269 Camp was Mansion Potton, near Potton, Bedfordshire.

Ravensden: In September 1945, five of 72 PoW Camp's satellite hostels contained Italian PoW residents, including one at Ravensden. The WLA had used Ravensden House, Wood End, Ravensden. In June 1946, the hostel was occupied by German PoW.

Roxton: By 30 March 1946, only 72 PoW Camp and Roxton Hostel were still being used for PoW. It was described as the oldest satellite hostel of 72 PoW Camp. Roxton Hostel had closed by May 1947.

Saffron Walden, Essex: On 14 April 1945, No. 607 IWC was at Hutted Camp, Ickleton Grange, Ickleton. Saffron Walden, Essex, existed under the command of 9 Group, Pioneer Corps.

Sandy: On 14 April 1945, No. 583 IWC was in the Hutted Camp, Sandy, Bedfordshire. The location of this was between St Neots Road and London Road (A1). The PoW from here possibly worked at ammunition dumps somewhere in Sandy itself. This became a DP camp and may not have been used by German PoW.

Stagsden: On 30 December 1943, there was a proposal submitted to build a new hostel at Stagsden.

Tempsford: In May 1947, PoW from Ducks Cross were located in a satellite camp at Tempsford. This would appear to have been a tented encampment upon what is now Tempsford playing field. By the following month it housed 432 German PoW.

Woburn: On 30 December 1943, there was a proposal submitted to build a new hostel at Woburn.

On 15 November 1942, the accommodation at 72 PoW Camp, Ducks Cross, was full, holding its War Establishment of 750 PoW and two officers (probably a doctor and a priest). An extension to the camp was proposed on 6 March 1943. By 12 January 1943, satellite hostels for 72 PoW Camp had been proposed at Woburn Road Ampthill, Highlands Farm, and at Godmanchester.

On 30 December 1943, there was a proposal submitted to build new hostels in 1944, at Biggleswade, Woburn and Stagsden. Strangely, 72 PoW Camp had vacancies for 538 PoW at this time. It may have been that the intention was to board out all the Italian PoW and use 72 PoW Camp for anticipated German interns only. As these hostels were not mentioned subsequently, the presumption is that they were not opened.

Initially, each PoW Camp operated individually, reporting directly to its local command. In the case of Bedfordshire this was Eastern Command. This command structure was later regionalised, so by 14 April 1945, HQ 9 Group, Pioneer Corps, commanded units locally.

On 16 May 1944, it is recorded that neither 72 Camp nor any of its satellites had become Italian co-operator camps.[30] As a result, the Italian PoW were to be replaced by Germans. However, by August, when 72 PoW Camp had become a German Working Camp, some Italians remained in hostels, apparently having then opted for co-operator status after all.[31]

With peace came time for the repatriation of German PoW. None of those in the Bedfordshire camps had been identified as potential war criminals so they were slowly released. Some returned to Germany while others remained in Britain as Displaced Persons, their pre-war homes being behind the Iron Curtain. They joined other DPs and demobilised servicemen in providing Bedfordshire with the labour force of the future.

Some PoW camps and hostels were closed; others, such as Ducks Cross, were retained as housing for DPs and other refugees. By 30 March 1946, only the main camp and the Roxton hostel were still being used by PoW; the remainder had closed.

Once the needs of the DPs and refugees ended, the government disposed of the camps. Private premises used for hostels were de-requisitioned. Removable assets were disposed of at government auctions. Some, like

Highlands Farm, became derelict before being refurbished. Ducks Cross site is now known as Dacca Farm, a collection of decaying Nissen huts and more modern buildings, supporting a number of light industrial facilities and a few residences. Interestingly, the latter appear to have been built, or converted, upon the ablution block sites, presumably because of the mains facilities available.

CHAPTER 3

Camp Life

Recorded in the last chapter were the camps and hostels that were opened to hold Italian and German PoW working parties across Bedfordshire. However, what was life like for those housed in them?

The Second World War was the first European war to be fought after the signing of the Geneva Convention in 1929. The Convention ruled on every part of the way a PoW was officially treated while in captivity, and Great Britain was very conscious of being seen to be scrupulous in its application.[32] The British Forces had their own instructions as to how PoW camps were to be administered and treated. These were published as part of Army Council Instructions.[33] Every camp had a set complement of staff and prisoners laid down by the War Office. This was known as its War Establishment (see Appendix 2).

All camps were open for inspection by the International Committee of the Red Cross. These visits were made on behalf of the prisoner's 'Protecting Powers' under the Geneva Convention. (See Appendix 3 for an inspector's report details on Ducks Cross camp.[34])

The camps not only housed the PoW, but also their guards. Initially, the need to provide a guard for every ten prisoners in a working party placed undue strain on army units that provided the guard force within the vicinity. The need for permanent staff was recognised, both to reduce abstractions from the 'Field Army' units, who could use the time more profitably, and to add professionalism to the guards. On 24 January 1942, Eastern Command transferred to the Pioneer Corps the cadre of soldiers at No. 1 Eastern Command PoW Cage at Dunstable. Thereafter the Pioneer Corps undertook national provision of soldiers. From the camp, working parties were dispatched by lorry. To alleviate the drain upon military resources no soldiers of combat fitness were posted to PoW camps. It was accepted that this policy might have posed a security risk. An official source stated: 'Most of the British personnel are of a low medical category and would be physically quite incapable of keeping up with these strong young prisoners.' Soldiers, however, were expected to 'take their coats off whenever possible to help [with agricultural work]'.[35]

Allocation of PoW labour was not a decision made by the camp commandant, but by the civilian Camp Labour Officer. He reacted, on behalf of the Ministry of Labour, to requests from employers submitted via the War Agricultural Executive Committee. Overseeing this process regionally was a Camp Liaison Officer.[36] However, having an army officer as camp commandant and a civilian responsible for allocation of work could lead to conflict. On 16 March 1943, a letter was sent, 'in the interest of better efficiency', from the Ministry of Labour to the War Office reminding camp commanders of the equal status held by the Camp Labour Officer.[37] Most camps, however, had good management relationships.

While the majority of PoW were sent out to work, a small number were retained to undertake the domestic chores necessary for the efficient running of the camp (see Appendix 4).

Food for camp residents was prepared by PoW cooks. The rations were prepared in kitchens within the camp. They initially received the same weekly rations as British soldiers: 42 oz of meat, 8 oz of bacon, 5½ lb of bread, and 10½ oz of margarine as well as vegetables, cheese, cake, jam and tea. This ration scale was changed very soon after the arrival of the first Italians as a result of observations made during ship journeys from North Africa to the UK: 'Compared with the British soldier, the Italians preferred more bread (preferably loose and not tinned loaves) and less meat; he liked vegetable soup and macaroni.' Italian PoW preferred quantity to quality and 'would only eat porridge if hungry'. It recommended that their diet be changed to include more bread and vegetable soup, as this was cheaper than the army depot diet.[38]

On 30 October 1942, Eastern Command responded to a request for reconsideration of an increased ration allowance for Italian PoW working in excess of an 8-hour day by saying it was neither necessary nor desirable, since the current scale of rations was adequate. It noted that in some camps, commandants were able to under-draw the Ration Cash Allowance without difficulty in spite of the large purchases of bread.[39] These rations were increased slightly in June 1945. An Italian PoW stated that while in South Africa they lived upon lentils, while in England they had 'everything to eat'. He was invited to eat Sunday lunch with a family and was given 'potatoes, peas etc.', but what he really wanted was pasta.[40]

For most prisoners there was little spare time: evenings, Saturday afternoon and Sunday. A letter on 31 May 1942 from Eastern Command identified that Italian PoW were adept at basket making and recommended that this be made an official spare time occupation, which, if sold for 1/-

The camp kitchen.

The interior of a PoW hut.

The mess hut.

each, would provide extra welfare funds. It is not known if this received official sanction.[41] More craftwork was reported on 21 November 1942 by Eastern Command, with Italian PoW making aluminium rings from the necks of water bottles that had been part of their equipment when captured, to give as gifts to local ladies.[42] The Germans also proved themselves adept craftsmen, capable of producing, from scraps, wooden children's toys, wheelbarrows, doll's houses and trains. Slippers were also made from string.

Surviving photographs of the camp show that the Italian prisoners found enough spare time to cultivate ornate gardens in the camp compound, constructing flowerbeds and what appear to be fountains.

Music was another means of suppressing boredom. The following quote comes from a report by a Red Cross representative in July 1945 (see Appendix 5): 'This is a camp with a vigorous community life. Everyone in the compound with whom I spoke, at once asked if this was not the best camp I had seen. The church was lavishly decorated in a colourful, Italianate way, the theatre also has every square inch painted by the Italians who were there, and even on the doorways of the dining room appear rather humorous cartoons. Many of the blackout boards have country scenes painted, with groups of cows and other animals. There are two orchestras, one with six camp-made mandolins, another with three violins, two saxophones, and accordion and cello. I attended a very good concert and heard the choir sing excellently. I give these details, which are really outwith the purpose of my

Above: The camp garden and huts.

Left: The camp garden fountain.

The camp garden pond.

visit, but they give the tone of everything in the camp ... One cannot help feeling in this camp that a great number of men will leave it better prepared for their future life, both technically and psychologically.'[43]

Yet again photographic evidence survives of a camp concert and dance band, The Blitzkriegs. These images show the musicians to be a mixture of prisoners and their uniformed guards. Occasionally dances were held in the camp to which local women were invited, and attended.

The performing arts were further encouraged by the formation of a theatre group in Ducks Cross camp. It is recalled that one of the British officers was so enthusiastic about promoting these shows he actually travelled to London to hire costumes on behalf of the cast.

Maintaining morale among the PoW was considered important. On 11 June 1942, Eastern Command suggested to the War Office that photos be taken of Italian PoW and sent home to Italy to demonstrate to their families the satisfactory conditions they were kept in.[44] Communication with home was encouraged, with the staff taking an interest in ensuring this happened. An example of this is a report dated 19 August 1942, when Eastern Command informed the War Office that twenty-three Italian PoW at one camp had received no letters from their family since capture and requested that enquiries be instituted to remedy this.[45]

Not all prisoners could cope with captivity and separation from their homelands. Sadly, a few died in captivity, some as a result of illness or accident, others by their own hand. (See Table 1 for those originally buried in Bedford Cemetery. Other men may be buried elsewhere in the county. It is believed all Italian and German deceased have been re-interned by the Commonwealth War Graves Commission post-war.)

The Blitzkriegs' four-piece band.

The Blitzkriegs' large concert group.

TABLE 1

Prisoners of War Buried in Bedford Cemetery.[46/47]
(Author cannot locate Heningford. 141 PoW Camp was at Beeson House Camp, St Neots, Huntingdonshire.)

Date died	Surname	Given name	Age	ID No.	Camp
24/11/1942	BRACCO	Eugene	24	49465	Ducks Cross
10/07/1943	AMEDEO	Antonio	23	T/49901	Ducks Cross
27/08/1943	SAPIA	Philippo	25	T/39033	
20/07/1944	BURONI	Pietra	28	T/54154	
18/08/1945	BARTOLI	Angelo	35	B/169218 (Carabiniere)	644 IWC
11/09/1945	FLEISCHMAN	Hans	43	B/169218	
25/08/1945	LUCKEY	Franz	20	979073	
26/10/1945	HORSCHEWSKI	Bernhad	38	A979259	
02/11/1945	POHL	Fridolin	45	B/76207	269 PGWW, Potton
23/09/1946	SCHERZ[48]	Herman	?	B302475	Ducks Cross
02/10/1946	GAEBEL	Gustav	40	B/24023	
10/10/1946	SCHADOW	Werner	?	A815742	Ducks Cross
17/01/1947	RUF	Alfred	45	A955788	Ducks Cross
16/03/1947	SILBERNAGEL	Ludwig	33	B188102	141 PoW Camp Heningford, Hertfordshire
30/05/1947	GREMARNS	Martin	26	AA053228	PoW Camp, Little Brickhill, Buckinghamshire
26/07/1947	SHULZ	Bruno	20	?	PoW Camp Ampthill
17/08/1947	GORRAN	Alfred	21	B732805	Whaddon Hostel, Whaddon, near Bletchley
20/10/1947	LIZEBA	Willi	20	A976983	278 PoW Camp, Clapham

At the camps there were lectures, concerts, gardening, handicrafts, sports and games. Many PoW took lessons in English or other educational courses. Some camps had their own magazines to supplement the official German-language newspaper; many were apparently printed in Luton.

Despite public complaints to the contrary, PoW received no preferential treatment to the civilian population. Eastern Command Order 964 of 1942 directed that two coal and cokeless days a week be instituted in every unit or establishment, these days being Wednesday and Sunday. Since the latter was a rest day, when PoW were likely to be in their huts and the only day personal washing could be done, another day could be substituted in PoW camps.[49]

The behaviour of Italians was originally exactly what was expected and the requirement for less stringent supervision was recognised. Accordingly, changes were instigated. On 20 February 1942, the Home Office wrote to all police chief constables. Only part of the letter survives, but from it can be ascertained the main changes:

> I am directed ... to inform you that recently some modifications have been introduced into the conditions under which Italian prisoners of war are employed as agricultural workers.

> 1. In some areas Italian prisoners of war are taken out in small parties from their camps during the day to work with individual farmers without military supervision. They are collected again in the evening and taken back to their camps.

> 2. In addition to the camps mentioned in the circular of the 9th September hostels are now being established in different parts of the country in which carefully selected Italian prisoners of war are housed – about 50 at a time – under the supervision of a military guard. From these hostels the prisoners, who wear a distinguishing uniform, are taken out or sent to work in parties without any military supervision, but during black-out hours they are generally locked in their hostel. On the prisoners' rest day they are restricted to the area within a short distance of the hostel, and are not allowed to go into houses, shops or public houses, or to post their letters at local Post Offices, or to fraternise with members of the public; local arrangements are made where possible for the prisoners to attend Mass, and walks are allowed.

> 3. A scheme is also in operation under which carefully selected Italian prisoners of war may be billeted individually with farmers. In such cases the prisoners are not allowed to leave the land of the employing farmer except to attend religious services, and are not allowed to fraternize with members of the public or go out of ...'[50] [remainder missing]

On 12 November 1942, yet more relaxation was made of the controls exerted over Italian PoW.

With reference to the Home Office circular 863,911/2 of the 20th February last, I am directed by the Secretary of State to inform you that it has been decided that the lorries in which Italian prisoners of war are taken to their work from prisoners of war camps may be driven by selected prisoners who have passed a driving test arranged by the War Office. An armed escort will sit in the driver's cabin. The responsibility for the behaviour of these prisoners will continue, of course, to rest with the War Office, and no action should be taken to apply to them Article 2 of the Aliens (Movement Restriction) Order, 1940; nor should any notice be taken of the fact that these drivers do not possess either a driving licence or a War Office permit in lieu. The Ministry of Agriculture will accept full responsibility for operation of these vehicles, including all accident claims.

In certain areas prisoners housed in camps and hostels are now permitted, if their previous behaviour has been good, to cycle to and from their work unescorted within a radius of seven miles from their camp. The employing farmer will inform the Commandant if such prisoner fails to arrive within half an hour of the due time, and the Commandant of the camp or officer in charge of the hostel will institute a search if any prisoner has not returned at the agreed time. During working hours the employing farmer will be responsible for the safe custody of the bicycles and for seeing prisoners do not get access to them.

Wherever this arrangement is put in force, the Commandant will inform the local Chief Officer of police. In these cases also no account should be taken of Article 2 (Movement restriction) Order, 1940.

Italian medical officers and chaplains are allowed out of prisoner of war camps on parole unaccompanied for exercise purposes on the following conditions:

a. They will be in uniform.
b. They must not fraternize with members of the public or engage them in conversation.
c. They must not go more than a mile from the camp.
   If any breach of condition (b) or (c) is observed the prisoner should immediately be brought back to the camp and the circumstances reported to the Commandant.[51]

The requirement for officers and chaplains to be in uniform is worthy of comment. A Red Cross report on officers clothing in 13 PoW Camp dated November 1941 recorded, 'The officers have still not received the uniforms asked for from Italy. After their capture the officers were able to buy civilian clothing. The military authorities are now offering them at a price more reasonable than that of good civilian clothes, a uniform similar to that of service dress (tunic and trousers) of British troops but dyed chocolate colour (the same colour as that of the battle-dress delivered to Italians in the agricultural camps.) This uniform, reserved exclusively for officers, does not bear any marking and it represents a good warm clothing.'

In December 1942, leaflets P.W.1, P.W.2 and P.W.3 were officially produced to provide information to farmers (see transcripts in Appendix 1). These provided guidance on how PoW should be treated.

Conditions for those Italians who were re-designated as co-operators were relaxed on 23 August 1944.[52] An explanation of the reasons for granting them privileges was given by the Secretary of State for War in answer to a Parliamentary Question on 14 November 1944:

> Prisoners of war may only be employed on limited types of work. It was therefore decided to take the opportunity offered by the Italian Armistice to accept certain of the Italian prisoners of war as volunteers for employment. I understand that on the average their output is higher than that of ordinary prisoners of war. They have eased our manpower difficulties and their work has been a valuable contribution to the war effort. It seamed only reasonable to grant to these men certain privileges not available to non-Co-operators.

These privileges included additional mail home and more freedom of movement outside of the camp during their free time, including visiting cinemas. Co-operators could arrange for the transfer of their earnings to Italy (but at a very poor exchange rate!). Their uniform was altered to give a less prison-like appearance, including 'ITALY' shoulder titles similar to those issued to British troops. Thereafter, Italians were seen frequently in Bedford without escort.

The arrival of German PoW in Britain created its own problems. Following the capitulation of Italy, Germans had fought both Italian and British troops in Italy. Italians were, therefore, now PoW in both Britain and Germany. Potential friction between Germans and Italians was sidestepped by strict separation of working gangs, a policy applauded by farmers among whom it was widely held that a single German was worth a dozen Italians.[53] This policy, however, does not seem to have been universally applied.

It is also interesting to observe the difficulties encountered when saluting was required. War Office Instructions, dated 20 January 1942, gave directions for saluting by enemy PoW: 'Italian & German will salute

Italian name badge to be worn on the arm of Italian PoW uniform.
(*Jon Mills*)

Imperial Officers [British and Commonwealth] by bringing the right hand
to the headdress.' Eastern Command HQ lodged protests against consent
being given for Italians, not wearing headdress, to give the Fascist salute,
while rules differed for German PoW. Those Germans 'not wearing headdress come to attention, or when on the move bring head and eyes to left
or right'.[54]

Towards the end of the war, the Political Warfare Executive (POWE)
was tasked with the re-education of German PoW. As with other types of
propaganda, POWE used the 'white', 'grey' and 'black' classifications for
German PoW. Prisoners classed as 'black' were considered dangerous ardent
Nazis, with 'good Germans' classed as 'white' and regular non-political or
easily led soldiers classed as 'grey'. White and grey category prisoners were
allowed to work with pay. For this they received *Lagergeld* – money for use
inside the camp, PoW were not supposed to receive Sterling.

The PoW were expected to undergo the POWE programme of re-education
to prepare them for a new life. Understanding democracy was supposed to
be the key to future German democracy.[55] Re-education of Germans was
based upon Vansittart's writings: 'it is an illusion to differentiate between the
German right, centre, or left, or the German Catholics or Protestants, or the
German workers or capitalists. They are all alike, and the only hope for a
peaceful Europe is a crushing and violent military defeat followed by a couple
of generations of re-education controlled by the United Nations.' Newsreels
showing concentration camps were shown, though some prisoners thought
they were just propaganda. Camps were periodically inspected to assess the
'colour' of the occupants (see Appendix 5).

For German PoW who were identified as having future leadership
potential, special courses were held at Wilton Park Estate, near Old
Beaconsfield, Buckinghamshire. From 1942, it had been used to
interrogate high-ranking Axis PoW. Interrogations ceased in 1945 and the
camp was taken over by the Foreign Office as a centre for de-Nazification
of German PoW.

In October 1947, a Foreign Office file recorded that 'anti government sentiment amongst civilians in this very rural and rather conservative district, tend to undermine the approach to a belief in democratic ways'.[56] The reference was not to Bedfordshire, but is indicative of the problems faced in re-educating PoW in areas where almost feudal life persisted.

Anthony Grenville later wrote: 'the record of the British in re-educating the PoW in their charge was thoroughly creditable. The official German history of German PoW in the Second World War explicitly acknowledges that Britain surpassed all other custodian powers in teaching PoW to respect democratic values and humane standards of behavior.'[57]

Post-war, *The One That Got Away* dramatised the story of the only German known to have escaped the Western Allies and successfully returned to Germany. The book[58] and subsequent movie, starring Hardy Kruger, concentrated upon one man, Franz von Werra, who escaped from a Canadian camp.[59] In reality, escape attempts by German PoW were as common as that of Allied prisoners in Germany. The difference was the success rate. Escape from island Britain was destined to fail. The English Channel was a very effective moat.

Early in the war, German PoW were mainly young men who had been brought up indoctrinated by Nazi ideology. Their morale was good and they believed that the forthcoming invasion of England would bring about their release. Therefore, they could see no reason to attempt escape.[60] With the prospect of invasion diminishing, a few serious escapes were organised, such as that planned at Devizes, Wiltshire, in December 1944. Mass escapers in the camp planned to form a hostile column fighting within England. On 24 December, Intelligence had warned of possible mass escapes from German PoW camps. Additional pickets were found and guards were warned to challenge only once, and then shoot. The numbers of reported escapes during the run up to the discovery of the Devizes plot gives some indication of the level of escaping in Britain at that time (see Table 2).

During 1945, a total of five German PoW were shot in British custody.[61]

Much credit for successful Allied home-runs must go to the assistance provided by the resistance movements and heroics of the population in the occupied countries. Despite all the friendliness of the British public they never provided an escaping prisoner with sufficient support during hostilities. Towards the end of the war, there was connivance in breaking the rules, as demonstrated by a German PoW. Having married a British war-widow while still a German PoW at Ducks Cross Camp, he was transferred to the Ampthill hostel. He maintains he escaped every night in order to spend time with his wife, cycling back to camp before morning roll-call.

TABLE 2

Reported Escapes of Prisoners of War in 1944.
(Compiled from entries in the War Diary of HQ North Lincolnshire Sub District.[62])

Date escaped	Camp	Escapers	Date re-captured
01/12/44	17 PoW Camp, Lodge Moor, Sheffield	1 German PoW	03/12/44
05/12/44	Farm at map reference 63/190250	2 Italian PoW	06/12/44
09/12/44	Marbury, Cheshire	4 Special Class German PoW	10/12/44
10/12/44	193 PoW Camp, Madeley Tile Works Camp, Madeley, Crewe	2 German PoW	Unknown
11/12/44	81 PoW Camp, South Hostel, Keadby, Scunthorpe	1 Italian PoW	Unknown
13/12/44	5 PoW Camp, Swanick	2 German PoW and 3 Dutch PoW	Unknown
15/12/44	PoW Camp, Sheffield	1 Special Class PoW	17/12/44
16/12/44	Detention Room, Sheet Camp, Ludlow	1 Italian PoW	20/12/44
18/12/44	194 PoW Camp, Council Houses Camp, Penkridge, Staffordshire	10 German PoW	20/12/44 (2) 20/12/44 (4) 21/12/44 (4)
20/12/44	17 PoW Camp: Lodge Moor Camp, Sheffield	6 German PoW	21/12/44
22/12/44	Pool Park Camp, Rughin	1 Italian PoW	Unknown
30/12/44	138 Italian Lab Company	1 Italian PoW	30/12/44

That a German in PoW uniform could travel throughout Bedfordshire without attracting attention reveals how, like the Italians before him, those Germans who had not abused the trust put in them were gradually permitted more freedoms and did not attract undue public concern. Even Germans who still professed a 'black' attitude could be found working unguarded in post-war Bedfordshire.

One Bedfordian asked a German, 'Don't you want to escape?'

'No. I'd lose my privileges,' he replied.[63]

Every German PoW was interviewed to determine their suitability for repatriation. This was determined by length of imprisonment, compassionate grounds, and political reasons. The first mass repatriations took place in 1946, the last in 1949. The methods utilised were not always seen to be fair, with complaints of Nazi supporters being released earlier than 'white' anti-Nazis. Some Germans could not be repatriated as their homes were within the Russian Zone. They joined the ranks of the Displaced Persons gathering in Britain.

CHAPTER 4

The Tilbrook Incident

On 16 November 1943, the *London Gazette* announced the award of the British Empire Medal (Military Division) to Private John Michael Shelton, Home Guard (Pertenhall Beds), 'in recognition of gallant conduct in carrying out hazardous work in a very brave manner'.[64] Such an award is extremely unusual, so what had John Shelton done to merit it? The citation provides a little more detail.

On Friday 9th July 1943 Antonio Amedeo, an Italian prisoner of war, escaped from a working party by killing a guard with a hedging hook. He took possession of the guard's service rifle and ten rounds of ammunition. Armed parties of soldiers, Home Guards and police carried out a search of the district from shortly after the escape until early afternoon of 10th July but the escaped man was not found. At about 6 p.m. on 10th July the escaped man entered a house, occupied by Private Shelton and his family, and helped himself to a meal. During this time the occupiers were also having a meal and the escaped prisoner, having finished his, passed into the passage of the house with a rifle in his hands and came face to face with Private Shelton, who had entered the passage from another room. The escaped prisoner immediately fired at Private Shelton and narrowly missed him. He then raced upstairs. Private Shelton instantly went up another staircase and worked his way along the landing until he located the escaped prisoner in his sister's bedroom, in a position from which the Italian could cover anyone coming up the main staircase. In spite of this Private Shelton entered the room and, with his service rifle, shot the Italian through the chest. Private Shelton was confronted with a situation where there was no time to ask for orders from his superior in the Home Guard. He showed marked initiative, personal courage and presence of mind, backed by sound training and thus gave an outstanding example of the way a Home Guard should behave in a situation of this kind.[65]

The award of the BEM to John Shelton relates to the only occurrence I can trace of a member of the Home Guard exchanging small-arms fire with the enemy on the UK mainland, although anti-aircraft units regularly fired at aircraft and flying bombs. This incident is therefore worthy of detailed examination in itself. It can also help to chronicle PoW's working lives and shed light upon the circumstances in which Private Hands was murdered.

Local newspaper articles[66] from July 1943 reported the proceedings at the Coroner's Inquests held regarding both the men who had died the preceding weekend. That of Private Hands was held at St Neots Magistrates Room on Tuesday 13 July. Major James Andrew McDonnell identified Private Hands, twenty-five years old, from 101 Hornsey Road, Anfield, Liverpool, a married man and father of one. An inquest upon Amedeo was opened at Kempston Police Station on Monday 12 and adjourned until Thursday 14. Lt Leslie Charles Rogers, Pioneer Corps, from the PoW Camp, identified Antonio Amedeo, who had been born on 21 January 1920 in Calabria, and taken prisoner at Tobruk. Major Charles Unwin Gregson, RAMC, gave evidence, having examined Amedeo's body and found gunshot wounds to the head, chest and thighs.

From the reports it can be summarised what had occurred. Just after 4 p.m. on Friday 9 July, Miss Rita Higgins (or Sylvia Rita Higgins), who was serving with the WLA, was hoeing sugar beet in a field near Tilbrook, Huntingdonshire, when she saw an Italian PoW jump over a stile. She noticed that he was carrying a rifle, which he proceeded to load. When he started to walk towards her she screamed and made towards her bicycle. She heard the rifle go off, but being unhurt fled to raise the alarm. An hour before she had seen the same prisoner following her across nearby fields. He had spoken to her in Italian, but thinking him lost she had directed him towards a temporary camp on the farm. Antonio Amedeo was this prisoner. Amedeo made good his escape into surrounding fields.

Miss Higgins' uncle, Alfred Higgins, also gave evidence. Earlier, at 3.45 p.m., he had seen two Italian PoW talking to their guard, identified as Private Hands, in nearby fields. Private Hands was guarding a working party of seven prisoners from Ducks Cross Camp.

They were working under an Ouse Catchment Board foreman labourer, Benjamin Cooper, hedging and ditching. Subsequent evidence was given that another group of prisoners had refused to work with Amedeo earlier and so he had come to work with Mr Cooper. Upon hearing the scream and shot, Mr Cooper thought that it was Private Hands firing at an escaping prisoner. Instead Private Hands' dead body was found, his head almost severed by a hedging hook that Amedeo had been sharpening earlier.

Private Hands had been armed with a service rifle and ten rounds of ammunition. As was customary, he would have left his rifle in a tent pitched nearby, de-activated. His rifle was found to be missing and the rifle's bolt and ammunition had been removed from its place of safety in his battle dress jacket pocket.

The alarm was raised and a search was instigated by the local Home Guard from Huntingdonshire and Bedfordshire, aided by two Bloodhounds: Worry and Jane. Huntingdonshire Police circulated the alarm. The search continued throughout Friday night and Saturday. By Saturday afternoon the only trace was a small wood fire found in hedges that was believed to have been the work of Amedeo.[67] (He is believed to have escaped into what was locally called Kimbolton Wood, Mile Ride, but is now known as Honeyhill Wood, Kimbolton Park. During the war this was several hundred acres of overgrown forest.)

Among the Home Guard who had been alerted were Bernard Sidney Shelton (or Sidney Shelton) and his eighteen-year-old son John. They lived, and farmed, at Grange Farm,[68] Pertenhall, Bedfordshire, about a mile from Tilbrook. John has stated that they had joined the search party, but had officially returned to their farm later. At about 6 p.m. John Shelton left the farmhouse sitting room with the intention of feeding the fowls, taking with him his Home Guard rifle. As he opened the door into a passageway the Italian, gun in hand, confronted him and, between two and five feet away, fired the rifle and missed. The Italian ran upstairs. John Shelton, together with his father, ascended another staircase. John found Amedeo in a bedroom and fired at him once. He was joined by his father, who, seeing foot movement beneath a bed, fired again. Amedeo was dead.

To obtain help, John Shelton then had to go to the parsonage and get the parson to make a telephone call. John did not know how. About six police cars later turned up. John Shelton recalled there was some sarcastic comment: 'For a day and a half we've been stuck out here on our own and now it's all over we've got lots of policemen all come in.' They took the body. No written statement was taken, but John went to Sharnbrook Police Station where, he says, he was 'done for Murder', but it was justifiable homicide. No post-incident support was available those days, but lots of VIPs came to shake his hand. John was back working the next day, carting flax, grown for parachute linen. He subsequently found the Italian's army boots outside the farm's dairy window, but, sadly, he said they were the wrong size for him.

When interviewed in later life, John Shelton recalled, 'I didn't feel very important about it. It's one of those things that happen. I'd just as soon it died quickly and been forgotten about. The Home Guard didn't really take part in any front line actions as far as I know, they didn't have any gallantry medals given them, so I suppose this was an unusual incident which is why they shouted about it.' He added, 'I was a kid, a young man, young for my age, in an unusual situation.' According to John, during the war his medal caused no stir as there were people with 'real medals, DFC [Distinguished Flying Cross] and such'.

John Shelton cannot explain Amedeo's actions. He had heard it said: 'He hadn't spoken to a girl for months. And Italians are a bit hot blooded they say. Land girls in the next field, "Can I have a chat with them?", "No you can't. Get on with your work." And he sort of blew his top. Other people say he was a charming young man, a very good pianist.' He remembers Italian PoW being used to clear weeds and overgrown bushes from brooks on the farm, always under an armed guard. 'They were harmless people really. Some of them were rather friendly really. We used to wave to them. They couldn't speak English and they [British] couldn't speak Italian.'[69]

Local rumour was that Amedeo had killed Hands because of the guard's refusal to allow the PoW to talk to the WLA girls, but there is no way that this information could have been ascertained, as the only two parties to the conversation were dead.

The story of Amedeo's break for freedom has also been retold in newspaper articles. 'Duel with a madman,' published by *Weekend*, in 1969, was based upon an interview with John Shelton.[70] While the storyline is basically correct it has been exaggerated. According to John Shelton it was over dramatised. This type of article helped perpetuate misconceptions.

I have wondered why an incident that apparently attracted such little national attention should result in the award of a medal from Great Britain's third highest tier. The fact that John Shelton showed the utmost bravery is undoubted, but why should this event be singled out from among the many other similar acts of bravery?

The sergeant in command of the local Home Guard was Mr Stewart Gordon Loch of Pertenhall Manor, known as Sergeant-General Loch, due to his retirement in about 1935, when he had held the rank of major-general following his service in the Afghan War of 1919. He was also colonel of Queen Victoria's Own Madras Sappers and Miners. This was a man who would have had the ability to write up a commendation for gallantry properly and possibly had the personal connections to ensure it was read.

Another factor might have been the official need to bolster recruiting in the Home Guard. The invasion fear had ebbed and many men felt the Home Guard redundant, leading to poor recruitment; compulsory enrolment commenced in July 1942. A hero, who had been seen to exemplify all that was good about the Home Guard's role, might help. However, highlighting the threat posed by having dangerous enemy soldiers living freely may well have caused any publicity to be perceived negatively.

The reason why Private Hands died has never been satisfactorily explained. A historian, Lucion Sponza, wrote, 'What happened that July evening resulted from an individual case of demented desperation, but also indicated that the mental condition of some prisoners had begun to waver.'[71] He does not support that comment evidentially, but it is credible; Amedeo's action was contrary to the pre-conceived Italian stereotype.

CHAPTER 5

Public Attitudes

Italian PoW arriving in Britain met a people whose thinking was already influenced by experiences and propaganda. The government, military and general public had pre-conceived ideas about the Italian. The Italian army was already considered less of a threat to Britain's internal security than the German armed forces. There was no public outcry against the Italians' arrival; even the trades unions accepted that they fulfilled a national need. Whereas Bedfordshire farmers, under the leadership of local landowners, had opposed the use of German PoW labour during the Great War, there was no such comment second time around.[72]

What exactly was the British perception of Italian PoW, and how did the British people come to adopt it? To understand this we first need to know something of the relationships experienced by the Italian and British people leading up to the arrival of the prisoners. Italy was a young nation; it had only achieved a unified nation status in 1870. Many British people had supported this process, taking Garibaldi to their heart. He visited Britannia Ironworks, Bedford, as a guest of James Howard in 1846, planting a tree that survived until it was cut down in 1943. Earlier, Italian art and culture had been celebrated and Italy featured in the 'Grand Tour' of the young elite of England. Italian architectural influences can be found throughout the major British country houses and state buildings. The perception of Italy therefore appears to be positive among the British upper classes, but what of the common man?

Nationally, the first Italian communities formed in Britain prior to the Great War with up to half a million immigrants arriving each year.[73] Many settled, grouped in the larger urban areas, but not in Bedford. They were subjected to prejudice and had trouble accessing the British labour market, so they identified niche markets they could thrive in: barbers, catering, and especially ice cream.

The Great War had provided the first opportunities for the British working class man to travel to Europe. Italy sided with the Allies but its armed forces failed to prove a match for those of the Austro-Hungarian Empire and Germany. This perhaps was the beginning of the tales of Italian army failings. British soldiers, including men of the Bedfordshire Regiment and Northamptonshire Yeomanry, reinforced the Italian front. These men witnessed the Italian people, military, and government at first hand and formed their own opinions of them, which they undoubtedly relayed home.

The rise of Mussolini in 1922 slowed the flow of economic migrants, but political refugees replaced them. The British public may not have appreciated this change at the time. In 1939, Bedfordshire had no large, recognisable Italian community. Zagatilli's, at 21 Elstow Road, was one of the first Italian shops in Bedford, selling ice cream.[74]

The local communities, therefore, had little first-hand knowledge of the Italian people, but they were subjected to other influences: primarily the press, radio and film. From the beginning of 1940, anti-alien sentiment had been fuelled by the Rothermere and Beaverbrook presses. Bosley wrote in the *Daily Mirror*, 'There are almost twenty thousand Italians in Great Britain. London alone shelters more than eleven thousand of them. The London Italian is an indigestible unit of population. He settles here more or less temporarily, working until he has enough money to buy himself a little land in Calabria, or Campagnia or Tuscany. He often avoids employing British labour. It is much cheaper to bring a few relations into England from the old hometown. And so the boats unloaded all kinds of brown-eyed Francescas and Marias, beetle-browed Ginos, Titos and Marios ... Now every Italian colony in Great Britain and America is a seething cauldron of smoking Italian politics. Black fascism. Hot as Hell. Even the peaceful, law-abiding proprietor of a back-street coffee shop bounces into a fine patriotic frenzy at the sound of Mussolini's name ... We are nicely honeycombed with little cells of potential betrayal. A storm is brewing in the Mediterranean. And we, in our droning, silly tolerance are still helping it to gather force.'[75] This sort of statement would not be acceptable today.

When Italy declared war on 10 June 1940, the country was seen as the junior partner in the Axis by many British people. Duff Cooper, Minister of Information, publicly attacked the shamefulness of Mussolini's declaration and, lumping all Italians together, accused them of cowardice and military incompetence in the First World War.[76] Sadly his biography makes no mention of what influenced his thinking.[77] There followed two nights of racially motivated public disorder directed at the Italian community nationwide, but not in Bedfordshire. This does not mean that the local feelings were any different from the rioters; there was just no target to vent them upon.

On 11 June 1940, Winston Churchill instructed the immediate internment of all male Italians – 'collar the lot' were the directions to police.[78] However, internment of Italian civilians was not an issue that directly affected the public in Bedfordshire either. When debating the concept of PoW labour in 1941, Winston Churchill wrote, 'It might be better to use these docile Italian prisoners of war instead of bringing in disaffected Irish over whom we have nothing like the same control.'[79] Churchill, therefore, indicated that he had a strong sense of what to expect from the PoW. We may not know what influenced him, but as the British leader and an accomplished orator, it seems unlikely his thoughts were out of kilter with those of the populace.

The army's officer class also held pre-conceived ideas. In an instruction manual distributed to Australian farmers one wrote:

> The Italian prisoner of war is a curious mixture, in that he can be made to give of excellent work if certain points are observed:
>
> 1. He cannot be driven, but can be lead.
> 2. Mentality is childlike; it is possible to gain his confidence by fairness and firmness.
> 3. Great care must be exercised from a disciplinary point of view for he can become sly and objectionable if badly handled ...
> 4. It is necessary that he be well and warmly clad, both in summer and winter ...
> 5. It appears that the Italian harbours no grudge or has no feeling of hatred for us as a race ...
> 6. A PoW if left to his own devices too long without constant supervision will tend to become lazy and loaf on the job, but this is readily cured by stricter supervision ...
> 7. The average Italian is keen on sport and likes nothing better than to go rabbiting (not with a gun).[80]

There is a lack of any specific recorded comment by the rank and file as to their thoughts regarding Italian PoW at this time, but the perpetuation of anti-Italian humour among the lower classes may be taken to indicate where their feelings lay. Richard Moore-Colyer writes, 'The victors themselves, or at least those of them on the home front, were generally unequivocal in their views of the Italian who were conceived as shiftless and dilatory, a sensual and excitable race whose enthusiasm for work closely paralleled their enthusiasm and stomach for fighting.'[81]

One of the few pieces of evidence referring to the army's attitude towards the treatment of PoW is found in secret papers prepared on 19 May 1941 by the staff of HQ 42 Division, stationed in East Anglia. It reported that Luftwaffe PoW who had landed in this country had 'been able to remain at large, sometimes for several hours, within the sight of troops, Home Guard and civilians. Sometimes they voluntarily surrendered to totally indifferent bystanders.' The file continues with further comments that PoW 'have been treated as benighted guests rather than enemies'. This document then gives instructions on the treating of PoW in the future, which, while not suggesting soldiers should physically ill-treat prisoners, suggested that the soldiers should 'act tough', adding, 'Kindness is wasted on German prisoners and is taken for weakness. The sooner troops learn that Germans only admire and react to strong measures and to discipline the better.'

However, the message did not appear to alter the actions of troops, for on 18 June a further admonishment followed: 'Any form of fraternisation with Prisoners of War tends to make them arrogant and difficult to control on arrival at hospitals ... Cigarettes and cups of tea will not be given to prisoners.' The same headquarters, reporting on 1 July 1941, had to then rein in their troops, recording, 'The need for an aggressive spirit and for the severe, but fair, treatment of German Prisoners of War has been stressed. It appears that some Commanding Officers have interpreted this policy as an authorisation to take no prisoners. This is entirely contrary to its intention.' I know of no evidence that indicates soldiers from 42 Division had unlawfully killed any German PoW.[82]

Confirmation of the story relating to the Luftwaffe PoW has been found in Suffolk Home Guard orders.[83] 'A wireless officer (in uniform) of a German night fighter which was shot down on 9th April [1941], according to his own account after the crash, was passed by a soldier who bade him "Good night" and then had to wait at a level crossing at which the gates were shut. The signalman eventually came to open the gates, but took no notice of him. Several other people did the same, and finally he was obliged to ask a civilian, in broken English, the way to a police station. The latter requested him to wait while he went round the corner to fetch a Home Guard who finally accompanied this PoW to the police station. The prisoner concluded that in these conditions parachute troops would have little difficulty in effecting a landing and carrying out their tasks.'

An unnamed RAF wartime author recorded, 'It has been said that part of the genius of the British in dealing with other races is their sense of impartial justice, understanding, and an ability to see the other man's point of view, without descending either to weak sentiment or to jackboot methods.'[84] Perhaps this may have an element of truth in it and the staff at 42 Division may have overreacted.

Wartime publications relating to Italians also used language that might be considered offensive, if not racist, by today's standards. An HMSO publication consistently refers to Italians as 'Wops'. The same author makes a personal observation about Italian prisoners. 'They complained bitterly about hard conditions ... pathetic people: one really has little time for them.'[85] Wartime diaries kept for Mass Observation, the social research organisation, also contain evidence of the public attitude towards Italy and Italians, as well as stereotypical insults about 'Wops' and their alleged lack of fighting potential.[86]

In an October 1941 letter to Lord Hailey, Margaret Read worried that 'nine tenths of the British population developed their views on the Empire from cinema, and ultra left wing propaganda of an anti-imperialist type'. Why should the population not have developed their views of Italians from similar sources? During 1940/41, fighting in the Western Desert resulted in the defeat of the Italian army, which was widely reported in the press. It provided a welcome counterbalance to the Blitz and other depressing Allied military failings elsewhere. Impressions of the Italian soldier were fixed in the public mind by newsreels at the cinema, and the showing of officially sponsored films such as *Siege of Tobruk, Desert Victory* and, in 1943, *Tunisian Victory*. Wartime films, whether feature, documentary or newsreel, while subject to the director's whim, towed the government's line. The public were allowed to see only what the censor and filmmaker wanted – positive propaganda. Denigrating the Italian soldier fitted this requirement. However, there were departures from this theme such as *Nine Men*, directed by Harry Watt in 1942, in which the Italian 'Macaroni Munchers' are not parodied but seen as worthy combatants.[87]

Ralph R. Donald writes: 'In American feature films, with the exception of Mussolini himself, the Italians were either ignored or received little serious criticism beyond their stereotypical lassitude and military ineptitude. By and large Italians were treated ... as buffoons, simple comic diversions in otherwise melodramatic scenarios.'[88] Donald also notes, 'During the formative years of motion pictures, the now-offensive image of the ignorant, happy, harmless, garlic-eating, wine-making, organ-grinding Italian had been frequently presented to American moviegoers.' While Hollywood productions, perhaps more than Ealing Studios, had been popular with British audiences before, during and after the war, all influenced the opinions of the British audiences. Irrespective of who produced the film, the vision of the Italian had been similarly disparaging.

Press comment varied during the war. In 1941, *Farmers Weekly* made almost no comment about the arrival of PoW. Adverse reporting gained momentum during the war, becoming most strident once the moment of crisis had passed and the work of Italian co-operators could be compared with German PoW. Whether this was due to selective reporting, censorship (official or otherwise), or due to a genuine increase in complaints is unclear. Some of it may be attributed to the relaxation of paper rationing, enabling papers to publish larger editions containing more reader's letters. Certainly the press had initially appeared to want to allay the public's fear of PoW. Photos appearing in *Farmers Weekly* showed soldiers guarding working parties with bayonets fixed. This was not a realistic portrayal of the guards, as we know from the inquests into Amedeo and Hands. After September 1944, increasing numbers of adverse comments resulted in the government attempting to persuade the press to take a less hostile line.

A photograph from *Farmers Weekly*. The official caption read, 'No happier crowd of workmen could be found anywhere in England, than the Italian prisoners of war at work in a barley field in the Home Counties. They sing while they work, while the farmer who owns the place, looks on approvingly. Some of the Italians are skilled workers. The only trouble is they can't speak English.'

From wartime files and press reports it becomes apparent that in the public's eyes, even before the offer of co-operator status, Italians were not meeting expectations. There was friction between the Italian PoW and the adult civilian population. But what exactly did the public expect from the Italian PoW?

A stereotype is usually based upon a group's factual common traits. Once identified, these traits are looked for in an individual's personality to establish if they fit the stereotype. Finding the common traits then reinforces the group stereotype and the perception. It is necessary, therefore, to examine individually the perceived wartime stereotype: the Italian soldier as cowardly and un-military; friendly to children and those who befriended him; amorous towards women; and a compliant, willing and capable farm worker.

COWARDLY

That the evidence of the attack by Amedeo upon Private Hands was a cowardly use of force is indisputable. However, the actions of one man do not confer similar status upon his compatriots. No evidence has been discovered to justify this allegation in relation to their time as PoW. On the contrary, Surgeon Lt Mario Constantine Lucchi, an Italian PoW, was presented with a Royal Humane Society parchment for rescuing one of two boys whose canoe capsized in the River Cam.[89] In 1942, the chief constable for the Isle of Ely reported two instances of Italian PoW reacting violently to provocation from a civilian labourer and to soldiers indicating their willingness to fight.[90] He also reported PoW attacking a child for making a 'Churchillian gesture'. The perception of a coward therefore remains.

UN-MILITARY

Were Italians really un-military? There was no opportunity to 'soldier' in the conventional sense as PoW, but the Italian army's record since 1848 was one of losing more battles than they had won. Mussolini's response to German complaints of Italian lack of dedication was that the Italian people were 'war-weary from long and exhausting colonial wars, and that too much precious blood had been spilled'.[91] This was probably the case as many conscripts had not seen home since 1937. Poor leadership, training and equipment led to poor morale and a lack of will to fight during the war's early years.

Barbara Wall recalled, 'As a land girl in 1943, I often came across Italian PoW working on farms here in England, all captured in the North African campaign. To a man, they told me they had made every effort to be taken prisoner in the hope of early repatriation.' A misguided hope as it turned out.

The British Command in North Africa were hard put to construct detention camps fast enough to cope with this avalanche of eager Italian prisoners, who were reportedly 'soon standing knee-deep in their own effluence'.[92] This may be considered harsh. The British army was not without its defaulters. Between 1941 and 1942, the British army had over 20,000 deserters in the Middle East alone. To counter this, in May 1942 General Auchinleck cabled the War Office suggesting the re-introduction of capital punishment, something that had been applied in the Great War and subsequently abolished.

The performance of Italian Partisans against the German army in Italy, post 1943, is evidence that the Italians could fight effectively if the cause was true to their heart. This would not have been anticipated by Britain in 1941. Perhaps some Italian soldiers felt affection for the British as a result of Great War comradeship and as a result did not wish to wage war against companions. This may also account for the friendliness some Italians showed towards the British people while in captivity and to escaped Allied PoW in Italy from 1943 onwards. The overall perception that the PoW was un-military remains unchallenged.

FRIENDLY

Before the introduction of billeting it was almost impossible for the general public to meet PoW unless they worked with them. Mrs Wilfred Percival was a frequent visitor and entertainer at PoW camps. Recalling her first attempts to gain access to Italian PoW, she said, 'it was the winter of 1943/44: a difficult period. Contact between prisoners and civilians was still "agin the law" and in some quarters even more "agin" public opinion.'[93]

Once the Italian became integrated into rural communities, attitudes changed. The British began to see that the stereotype did not apply. By December 1945, once repatriation had started, Mrs Percival believed that, 'In the small proportion of cases where men had been befriended by civilians, where they had been billeted at farms and got on well with the country-folk and perhaps fallen in love with the country lasses, we began to hear less comment as the time for departure drew near. But the softer verdict was always reserved for an individual, or a certain group of individuals; for the "publicco Britannico" there would be respect, even admiration, but also – at best – antipathy, and – at worst – something akin to hatred.'

It is possible that farmers' families showed Italian PoW the first acts of kindness they had experienced in many years. One Kempston farmer's son remembers Italian prisoners billeted in the same building as an evacuee family with two children without any problems. He speaks of Italian PoW as 'really nice tidy boys' who learnt English. He used to provide them with civilian clothing in order to take them to the cinema, contrary to the regulations.[94] An Irishman did a similar thing, taking them to a Bedford cinema in borrowed suits, to see *The Dawn Patrol*, but they started cheering for Germany and gave the game away.[95]

One Bedfordshire man recalls the Italians: 'As children we were told that we mustn't talk to them. I don't think they were allowed to [talk to us] at all first. They were soon allowed out. Particularly on a Saturday and Sunday I can remember them walking through and they'd stop and talk. We didn't understand what they were saying but they were so friendly. In that hostel on a Sunday afternoon they treated the local children to a film show. Half-way through they stopped and we were treated to a soft drink and a piece of slab cake. They were very generous.'[96] That said, it was reported that the WLA in North Lincolnshire were so frightened of unguarded Italian PoW in their proximity that it temporarily down tools.[97]

As mentioned earlier, basket- and ring-making were identified as an Italian PoW skill. Was the recommendation to the War Office that this be made an official spare time occupation merely a means to generate War Office income or was it intended to take control of the market away from the PoW? The latter would have distanced the PoW from the British. After the ring-making was reported in November 1942, Eastern Command requested to know if these water bottles should be collected as salvage and if so, should British-type water bottles be issued in lieu?[98] Why should the army want to withdraw the Italian water bottles and expend British resources to replace them? Perhaps they wished to remove the means of ingratiating the PoW with the public.[99]

The Italians did build positive community relationships. When some PoW declined co-operator status, Eastern Command received a letter from Cambridge alleging harsh treatment of other Italian PoW who had became co-operators. Mention is made of the damaging effect this had upon the Italian's attitudes and among the 'decent people of Cambridge who are feeling extremely indignant'.[100] Among some elements of British society, the Italian PoW had obviously won support for considerate treatment and were no longer considered enemies.

One Italian PoW billeted in Box End Farm, Kempston, recorded that 'the owner was like a father to me and I like a son to him'.[101] The prisoner traditionally rated family and friendship highly. This trait is one that probably most endeared the Italians to those who came to know them and supports the continuation of this strand of the stereotype.

AMOROUS

The Italian had a reputation as a lothario. One wartime schoolgirl felt that Italian PoW 'were so glad to get out of the theatre of war, not being natural fighters, so happy to be in Britain on farms'. They were attractive and outgoing. As a teenager she found them fun. She worked during harvest on Crowbourn Farm, Melchbourne, and used to take Italians their food. However, she was very glad to get away from them quickly as they were inclined to be amorous. She believes Italians left behind a positive legacy, as they were vociferous and fun, whereas Germans were not so communicative.[102]

The national policy was not to have Italians, Germans or the Women's Land Army working alongside one another, but this was not consistently applied. The Bedfordshire WLA were warned of the Italian PoW' reputation for womanising and were advised to go to toilets in groups of six for self-protection. The WLA also complained about inequality of treatment, such as luncheon facilities; the Italians got to eat food provided by the camp under cover while the WLA had to eat sandwiches brought from their hostel in the cold and wet.

Mrs Percival wrote in her autobiography: 'Because of the Southerner's instinctive inclination to the more sensual enjoyment of life; because the Italian co-operators were not prevented from meeting women at their work or being taken home by them and coming under the immediate influence of female attraction; because they were allowed to visit cinemas and suffer the disturbing excitement of sexy films; and more than all else, because some women seemed to enjoy prisoner baiting as a sport, whilst others fell sincerely and deeply in love with individual Italians and desired to marry them – with the approval of their families – the order concerning fraternisation appeared extremely hard to the co-operators themselves, and extremely unimaginative to all who had to contend with them, except the most stony-hearted. The co-operators penalty for consorting varied from six months to two years imprisonment, the women were not punished.' These comments have since been called 'an elaborate, condescending, defence of the passionate Italian temperament'.[103] Alternatively, Italian advances could have been misunderstood, resulting in a clash of cultures.

Not all women refused advances. In one Bedfordshire village it is recounted that the local men banned all Italian PoW from the community, following the pregnancy of two local women after illicit relationships.[104] The attraction of fit, young Italian men among a community where similar British men were absent at war has to be considered. The evidence supports the idea of amorous Italians, but could also be interpreted as having been sexual predators. The darker side is not recounted publicly and has not influenced the modern public image.

COMPLIANT

According to Bob Moore, comments abound about the Italians' usefulness and docility, although little contemporary empirical evidence was given to support that view.[105] However, there is evidence available to the contrary.

Blackmailing farmers by threats of poor productivity appears to have been common practice. Employers providing an unofficial productivity bonus of cigarettes or cash became the norm. Some farmers responded by breaching the law themselves, tending to bend the regulations in order to get the best from their PoW. In October 1944, PoW were reported to have refused to pick potatoes unless they were paid 4s a day and the farmer admitted paying them 3s a day in contravention of regulations.

On 14 December 1944, a War Office letter stated that such payments should not be paid and that farmers might give gifts to the camp welfare funds, but as such funds were already large this was to be discouraged. Prosecuting farmers was an option, but it was felt inappropriate; the authorities were 'doubtful of wisdom of giving the matter undue publicity in the local press, which it would seem would merely draw attention to the fact that such practice exists and would not necessarily have any deterrent effect, but would probably increase press criticism of the Italians'.[106] These are not the actions of docile men, but for the reasons stated they did not get publicity, and the British public remained unaware of the Italian's attitude.

When comparing the numbers of Italian PoW involved in agriculture with the known number of unpleasant incidents, the indication is that the majority of Italians did not overtly cause trouble. Were the Italians voluntarily compliant or behaving under duress? A prisoner found lacking in any respect could be returned to a PoW Camp, while a farmer losing vital labour encouraged other farmers to maintain discipline.

The IRCC reported: 'collective punishment relating to feeding has never been imposed at Ducks Cross: but as a tool for ensuring the compliance of prisoners it was obviously thought necessary by the British.'[107] One

Kempston farmer knew how to control his twelve Italian PoW. During their first week of work, whenever he visited the Italians he only ever found ten working; two were always at the latrine. At the end of the week he gave them only ten packets of cigarettes for the 'ten workers'. When they needed a hair cut the Italians went to an Italian barber in Bedford and spent the whole day chatting. The camp commandant sent them to the German barber next time. The Italians were back out in 5 minutes, with shaven heads, very unhappy. They got the message.[108]

One farmer's son remembers one German would not work on the farm so he was returned to the camp. There he was put to do the disliked camp chores. He was a changed man when next allocated to farming.[109] No doubt this form of attitude adjustment was also used upon recalcitrant Italians.

Despite the selection policy it is apparent that some fascists did end up in Britain and that they caused trouble. This may be inferred from an Eastern Command report dated 24 April 1942, which submitted a case regarding an anti-fascist prisoner in 26 PoW Camp (Barton Field, Ely) who was causing considerable trouble on account of his political sympathies. It was suggested that he be transferred to another camp in which other anti-fascists were confined.[110] Fascist prisoners were reported distributing fascist leaflets from the rear of the vehicles transporting them to another camp.[111]

Escape attempts by Italian PoW were frequent, despite always ending in recapture. Evidence of flouting of the lesser rules by PoW is abundant. On 25 July 1942, Field Security Section, 2 Corps, reported that there was considerable comment among troops and civilians on the liberty enjoyed by Italian PoW working for farmers in the area. The '2 Corps Area' included parts of Bedfordshire, Cambridgeshire and Suffolk. The report highlighted how difficult it was for the guards to oversee working parties and mentioned Italians being found wandering unescorted near aerodromes. The Deputy Air Provost Marshal RAF, No. 4 Region, reported that on 4 October 1942, RAF Police had stopped two Italian PoW near Fowlmere aerodrome in Cambridgeshire. The farmer responsible for the prisoners eventually collected them, but the RAF was particularly concerned as Duxford (Experimental) aerodrome was adjacent. The PoW were five miles from their billets instead of the regulation mile.[112]

However, some of the army's attitude to the expectations of the guard may have been at odds with those of the public and their fellow soldiers. On 26 May 1942, 8 Field Security Section reported that Italian PoW from Royston, who attended Adenbrooke's Hospital, Cambridge, each week for minor ailments, arrived and departed by train under unarmed escort. While waiting for the train they walked freely around Cambridge. Highlighting recent escapes of PoW, 8 Field Security Section thought it advisable to take greater precautions.

Not all soldiers were expected to guard diligently at all times. In September 1942, the commandant of an unidentified Eastern Command PoW camp admitted that his guard staff assisted farmers for payment, but maintained that such employment came within the provision of 'voluntary work'. Personnel concerned proceeded as escorts to the prisoners and, having delivered them at the various farms, were then granted permission to be 'off duty' until they were due to escort the prisoners back to camp in the evening – it was during this 'off duty' period that the escorts voluntarily assisted the farmers. Eastern Command considered this was legitimate practice and sought War Office consent for the arrangement to stand.[113] If the army set flexible standards then PoW breaking the rules should have been expected. After all, British PoW in Germany were at that time expected to make escape attempts.

Had Italian PoW at Ducks Cross camp actually matched the perceived stereotype, the majority of these 'compliant' men would be expected to have opted for co-operator status, but they did not. Why should Italians decline to become co-operators, when the new status offered preferential treatment? The answer to this question might lie in a June 1945 correspondence to the War Office from Patrick Donner, prospective Conservative candidate for Basingstoke. Referring to a letter received from a local National Farmers Union, 'farmers regretted Italian PoW not volunteering as co-operators but they believed it was because the PoW thought they would be removed from farms and made to undertake military work.'[114]

Initially, the Italian PoW were compliant, but when co-operator status and billeting made control of them more difficult they took advantage of the situation and slackened off. The prisoners were only compliant when they had to be. The earlier advice to the Australian farmers may have been beneficial. However, the authorities could not afford to be seen to admit publicly to the problem.

WILLING AND CAPABLE FARM WORKERS

Persistent complaints were made to the press of idleness among Italian PoW. Comment was made that British seamen risked their lives taking food to liberated Italy while the Italian PoW were doing 'by ordinary Englishmen's standards, one hour's work a week'.[115] Some farmers held that a single German was worth a dozen Italians.

Contrast this, however, with support expressed for the Italians prior to their arrival: 'Farmers, many of whom object to employing conscientious objectors are now asking to be allowed to use prisoners of war to help in work on their farms.'[116]

When billeting was announced, opposition from farmers and their families was reported in the national press. 'Why should our wives look after Italians?' ran the headline.[117] The article accused Italian PoW of being 'surly, bad-tempered and often cheeky' as well as being slow workers. The same newspaper also quotes Mr H. G. Saunders, County Executive of Hertfordshire: 'some of the Italians are very bad and some quite good. There are terrible tales told of the insolence of some of them.'

In 1942, Lord Somerleyton wrote to the East Suffolk Agricultural Executive Committee after observing a group of PoW who had 'only managed the work of two boys a day'. He wrote, 'These prisoners spend their time on setting snares and talking to children on the village green or go on strike for another blanket, so that they have more than our own men at the front.'[118] However, by 1943 farmers in Cumberland appreciated the work of 'cheerful, useful Italians, whom they considered more useful than half trained land girls incapable of heavy work'.[119]

On 20 March 1945, the Secretary of State for War, Sir James Grigg, was asked for his views when comparing Italian with German PoW as land workers. While maintaining he had a view, 'wild horses would not drag it from me.'[120] Were politicians also becoming wary of voicing support for Italians?

Despite negative reporting nationally related to agriculture, local feelings were different in the Bedfordshire brickworks. Towards the end of 1947, PoW made up nearly one-quarter of the whole labour force employed at Stewartby Brickworks. The nationality of the PoW was probably German. That of European Voluntary Workers was unspecified (see Table 3[121]).

TABLE 3

The Nationality and Numbers of Prisoners and Staff working at Bedfordshire Brickworks, 1947/48.

Week ending	Total staff	PoW	Polish	EVW	Eire
30/11/47	2,090	473	311	112	56
04/01/48	2,179	284	332	176	58
28/03/48	1,798	0	189	148	0

One local trade union leader later maintained PoW were the best workers the brick industry ever had. By 1948, the prisoner's contribution in the brickfields came to an abrupt halt.[122] No doubt the Italians were capable, when motivated, and the contribution they made to Britain's war effort is underestimated, but the type of work and level of supervision within the brickfields may have reduced their opportunities for shirking. There was no individual support for farmers wishing to retain their Italian PoW post-war.

Although the Italian PoW initially met the expectations of his captor, as the war progressed conditions changed. The Italian's attitude changed as did that of the British, both officially and socially. In August 1944, a Foreign Office file minute noted, 'It is not open to doubt that the ungenerous, procrastinating and equivocal policy adopted towards Italian Prisoners of War since the Armistice has had an alarming effect on their attitude towards this country, which has changed from a general willingness to co-operate to disillusionment, resentment and hostility.'[123] The Italians as a group did not match the stereotype consistently, but changed with circumstances.

Graffiti found on a roof tile while refurbishing the old Italian PoW hostel at Highland Farm may sum up the prisoner's feelings: 'It was a very hard life. Mario Ludovic, Good Friday, 19 April 1946.'[124]

Were similar attitudes held about the Germans? Britain's relationship with the Germans began long before the country of Germany was formed by unification in 1870. The bond between Germany and Britain has been perceived as genetic, social and religious. The Germans were Protestant unlike Britain's traditional enemy, France. Britain and the German state of Hanover were jointly ruled from the time of George I until the accession to the throne of Queen Victoria.

British and German soldiers fought together against Catholic rule and Napoleonic invasion, but fought against each other during the First World War.

It was perhaps the First World War that gave rise to the undercurrent of bitterness still simmering today on and off the football pitch. During The Great War, Britain suffered approximately 900,000 fatalities and 2 million wounded. This catastrophe was very much within living memory during the 1940s.

There was no serious governmental attempt at propaganda during the First World War in Britain. The theatre and press churned out patriotic and jingoistic print and music. It influenced public opinion about alleged German war crimes in 1914, some of which are still perceived as fact today. Bertrand Russell, the pacifist anti-war activist said that 'the sins of England [would] sink into insignificance beside the German treatment of Belgium'.

Following the sinking of the Lusitania in 1915, British public prejudice hardened, resulting in rioting and attacks on German owned premises.

Public pressure brought about internment of male enemy aliens. Even the army reformer and ex-Minister of War, Lord Haldane, was forced to resign as Lord Chancellor for a supposed pre-war predisposition towards Germany, such was the strength of feeling. Anti-German feeling voiced by the Suffragette leadership presumably helped influence the female perspective.

Well-known writers such as Arthur Conan Doyle and John Buchan wrote patriotic novels, such as *The Thirty-Nine Steps*, which are still read today. Rudyard Kipling's poem 'The Beginnings', published in 1917, clearly identifies that the English had learned to hate during the Great War. Writing the following year, he wrote: 'The Hun has been educated by the State from his birth to look upon assassination and robbery, embellished with every treachery and abomination that the mind of man can laboriously think out, as a perfectly legitimate means to the national ends of his country.' Having lost his only son in France he never forgave or forgot; every one of his post-war books had at least one war story or poem.

Kipling was far from being alone in these thoughts. Britain had been persuaded that Germany alone was to blame for the war. Even the Bishop of London is quoted as having preached, 'Kill Germans! Kill them, not for the sake of killing but to save the world. Kill the good as well as the bad … Kill the young men as well as the old … I look upon it as a war for purity'.

Junior officers, who were better educated and could afford publication costs, published the majority of wartime memoirs. It is from their writings that the feelings of the other ranks have been distilled. That opposing soldiers in the trenches held sympathies for each other is questionable, but British soldiers who had fought in the trenches, as opposed to rear echelons, did have a healthier respect and a less jingoistic attitude towards the capabilities of the German soldier.

Evidence of German PoW being well treated is available, but nobody ever evidenced to the contrary, and, therefore, the perspective is almost certainly distorted. What is undeniable is the way the other ranks held Prussians in more contempt than their attitude towards Bavarians and Würtemburgers. Identical opinions of Prussians may also be observed among the German population as a whole. Incidentally, the Germans held higher regard for Australians and Scots, and were more dismissive about the fighting abilities of the Welsh and County Regiments from Southern England.

The culture and music emanating from Germany had long been admired, but was discredited post-1914. During the First World War, classical scores by Germans no longer featured in concerts. There was, however, less anti-German hysteria between 1939 and 1945, when the arts were not suppressed; few worried that the BBC's victory anthem was actually Beethoven's 5th Symphony.[125]

In peacetime, in 1919, some leaders, such as Winston Churchill, had hoped to recruit the Germans to oppose Bolshevism, but the public's feeling was for vengeance. The 1918 General Election had ensured a government that would seek a harsh peace.

Not everyone continued to dislike the Germans, though. Pre-1939, the apparently successful re-emergence of Germany from the ruins of defeat and depression had impressed many. Sir Oswald Mosley led the pro-fascists in pre-war Britain in imitation of Mussolini and Hitler. Unlike France and America, Britain took a more lenient attitude towards the repayment of reparations and later to German re-armament. As Germany became more aggressive, the British government adopted the policy of appeasement, which appeared to be a good thing for all concerned.

The Austro-German *Anschluss* and the Czech Crisis were interpreted by some as German self-determination and a righting of the 1919 wrongs. The British public apparently knew no better and therefore accepted the politicians' word more readily than we might today. Led by Neville Chamberlain, the politicians gave in to German demands. An increasing number of British people began to voice disagreement though, and warned of the danger posed by Hitler to this country.

However, there was little in the way of fact upon which the public could formulate a view of the new Germans. Of the thousands of articles concerning Nazism appearing in the 1930s British press, not more than twenty-five actually sought to define, explain or analyse Nazi ideology. The Berlin Olympics of 1936 were well covered by the British press, but in such a manner as to avoid upsetting the Germans.[126]

After the First World War, the German population in Britain was reduced to 20 per cent of pre-war numbers. As a result of Nazi victimisation, about 70,000 German refugees entered Great Britain, of whom some 55,000 remained, the rest moving on to America and the Commonwealth. Automatic entry was refused to Germans, only 'distinguished persons' were admitted. This British policy ultimately led to the death of many unfortunate Jews. The influx of anti-Nazi Germans was certainly noticeable within British society, a feature not experienced before 1914 and the outbreak of the First World War.

There is a catchphrase: 'The only good German is a dead German.' Exactly how old this is is difficult to say, but its chilling humour needs little explanation. While the 'Phoney War' generated little in the way of hatred, the German invasion of France and the Low Countries during May 1940 resurrected all the venom of 1914. Allegations of atrocities were followed this time by evidence. The bombing of Rotterdam, the 'strafing' of refugees upon roads, and the 'unsporting' use a 'Fifth Column' brought the British press to full pitch. This in turn reinvigorated the British public's hatred of 'The Hun'. A 1941 quotation from the House of Commons supposed that there were 'less than seventy million malignant Huns, some of whom are curable and the rest killable'.[127]

Sir Robert Vansittart, a career diplomat, published an anti-German pamphlet in January 1941.[128] His antagonism towards the appeasement of Germany had brought him into conflict with the political leadership of the time and he had been removed as a Permanent Under-Secretary in 1938. He argued that all Germans were militaristic and aggressive, citing past German history. Demand led to ten reprints, indicating his pamphlet was widely read. How much the readership agreed with him is incalculable.

The Blitz had little direct affect upon Bedfordshire. Interestingly, the residual national memory refers to the Luftwaffe, with almost no mention of the Regia Aeronautica's (Italian air force) involvement. Both British and German governments anticipated that being bombed would break British morale. However, it was later reported that morale had actually risen in areas that had been regularly bombed.[129] It cannot be doubted that those directly affected felt animosity towards the bombers.

Pastor Bergmar Forell recorded in his diary, 'It seems that there is a distinct propaganda to make the whole German people out as criminals and sadists.'[130] The British certainly distinguished between German and Italian PoW. The German was considered ideologically committed and a dangerous opponent, the Italian was basically a simple peasant who had been led astray by Mussolini.

In March 1945, prior to 21st Army Group crossing the River Rhine into Germany, Field Marshal Montgomery published a letter to the army. 'It is too soon for you to distinguish between good and bad Germans; you have a positive part to play in winning the peace by definite code of behaviour. In streets, houses, cafés, cinemas etc., you must keep clear of the Germans, man, woman and child, unless you meet them in the course of duty. You must not walk out with them, or shake hands, or visit their homes, or make them gifts, or take gifts from them. In short, you must not fraternise with Germans at all.' These restrictions upon fraternisation in Germany were not relaxed until 6 August 1945.[131]

The liberation of concentration camps, such as Belsen in 1945, must have had an adverse affect upon public opinion of Germans. So far, there appears to be no evidence of it directly affecting the way in which PoW were treated. This may have been because the maltreatment in the concentration camps was blamed upon Nazis and few PoW openly admitted to those beliefs. It can be assumed that the German PoW did not fit the public expectation of what they would expect of a people capable of such horrendous crimes. To some extent they were correct, as very few German soldiers then in Britain would have been involved in the 'Final Solution'.

Within the brickfields it has been recorded that supervisors 'were stricter with Germans than they were with the Italians'.[132] The supervisors, of course, were older British men with longer memories than the younger women who had replaced the pre-war male workforce. These women took a softer attitude, as recalled by one worker. She remembers German PoW from Clapham were collected by the London Brick Company to work as 'setters and drawers' in brickworks. They were young, aged between fourteen and sixteen and some relationships flourished. The management frowned upon fraternisation and instructed the women to not talk to 'the enemy'. She was once suspended for three days for breaking this rule as she felt she couldn't be rude by ignoring PoW. They also played hide-and-seek' among the brick stacks, but never indulged in any 'naughtiness'.[133]

Few PoW spoke English upon their arrival, but some soon learnt it. Some Germans made up their minds not to.[134] The rebellious nature of German PoW was noted elsewhere in Britain. Every Sunday, 4,000 German PoW at Warth Mills Camp, Bury, Lancashire, stood in the open to sing strident Nazi anthems.[135] It was not quite the same at Ducks Cross. Their football team played other sides, including a civilian one from Great Barford that included a number of demobilised servicemen.

A WLA girl remembers that German PoW were not as nice as Italian PoW. 'I think they felt that we were the enemy and we tried not to have anything to do with them if we could help it.'[136] Other brick workers thought them 'not too bad. A lot of them didn't want to go back. Some of them were quite decent fellows, really. They were the same as us, weren't they, in a way.'[137] Not all was sweetness and light. While working on a haystack in Sharnbrook, one WLA land girl recalled having a very dramatic moment. While some older German PoW were wanting to show her family photos, a younger German attacked her with a pitchfork. Before injury was caused to her, another WLA girl, Mary McGuire, threw him off the haystack. He received injuries requiring hospital attention. The reason for the attack was thought to have been an attempt to obtain some lorry keys.[138]

Apparently many German PoW eventually came to terms with the British people. A survey in April 1948 found no evidence of positive hatred of the British by German PoW: 7 per cent disliked the British, 90 per cent were indifferent, but only 3 per cent positively liked them.

In April 1945, an article written by John Good in the *Sunday Express*, two weeks before the end of the war, said: 'The Germans are moral lepers and should be held as such until we are certain that the race has been expunged and redeemed.'[139] Some people were, however, willing to risk

Dedicated to F.C. Great-Barford in remembrance of the matches with No. 72 G.P.W. Camp, Colmworth.

Lockert, Maeuter, Kraemer, Stavermann, Frede, Schmittjes, Pieper Hahn, Hippe, Schaedlich, Meier, Petri ~ 1947 ~

The Ducks Cross football team.

catching 'leprosy'. Post-war, Tom Skeffington Lodge, Labour MP for Bedford (21 February 1946–15 December 1949), was keen to renew British friendship with Germany and paid regular visits to PoW camps. He ensured they were entertained at Christmas by British families.[140]

Indeed, many families were willing to offer the hand of friendship. This resulted in many long-lasting relationships, but not all were welcomed. When a local lady announced her intention to marry a German PoW she was ejected from the WLA hostel at Clifton. Her mother told her to have nothing to do with Germans as her father had been wounded during the Great War. She married him anyway and went to live in post-war Germany, returning to Britain in 1949: 'Even in those days there was quite a hatred against the Germans.' The local council refused to house them despite a doctor's letter supporting their application. They feel they were later passed over on the housing list. Time did not heal every old wound, however. Press reporting of their wedding anniversary fifty years later resulted in them receiving hate mail, calling her husband a Nazi.[141] This marriage proved to be the basis for the twinning of Great Barford with Wollstein, Germany, with many benefits to both communities.

Did the use of PoW affect the employer–employee relationship? Surprisingly, the use of alternative labour sources appears to have created little friction. In April 1941, instructions were sent to War Agricultural Executive Committees to cover the kind of work to be performed by PoW, suggesting they 'consult NFU and workers on the question of hours of work etc.; so as not to endanger the goodwill of our own workers and the farmers'.[142] The NFU recognised that the national need must prevail and accepted the new arrivals.

On 30 June 1941, official concern was expressed that unions may object to PoW working for contractors. To ensure a fair allocation, a civilian Camp Liaison Officer ascertained labour demands and allocated prisoner resources from the camps. Any Trades Union Congress objections to Italian PoW were not truly tested until January 1944, when suggestions were made of skilled Italians working beside, perhaps even replacing ordinary workers. Their employment in industry, either in a skilled or unskilled capacity, was then made dependent upon there being no British labour available, and upon no objection being raised by the local branch of the trade union concerned. In April 1944, when redundancy of labour in certain industries began to occur, steps were taken to ensure that Italian prisoners were not retained in jobs where suitable British workers were available.[143] These led to the blueprint for a series of post-war government-sponsored schemes aimed at the 'importation' of Italian industrial workers to Britain. It was under these schemes that Italians returned to work in Bedfordshire brickfields.

Foreign Office files dated October 1945 do, however, record that unions often complained that farmers specifically took advantage of cheap PoW labour.[144] In 1943, all PoW who were qualified agricultural workers received 1s per day and unskilled prisoners 6d. This was paid in tokens or credited to savings accounts that could be used to purchase luxury goods. Farmers paid the War Office 48s per week per unskilled man (37s if billeted). By comparison, civilian agricultural labourers wages were 60s per week rising to 70s per week by 1945. This disparity does not appear to have ever caused serious labour relation problems, unlike in Australia where farms employing Italian PoW were blacklisted by unions. Some discontent was experienced when prisoners, having saved more than the civilian farm labourers, amassed £600–£800 in credits, wished to purchase items that were unaffordable by civilians or guards.[145]

Upon the announcement of the hostel scheme there had been some adverse press reporting after farmers in Worcestershire, Hertfordshire and Buckinghamshire complained to their War Agricultural Executive Committees.[146] Their wives resented the additional cooking and domestic chores associated with resident PoW together with the security implications.

Some farm workers had complained that the PoW were provided with rubber boots, while they had to provide their own using clothing coupons. In reality, the War Agricultural Executive Committees provided rubber boots for all staff engaged on drainage work. However, to obtain free boots civilians had to make a long-winded application process. Once, when the clay pits at Kempston Hardwick flooded, German PoW refused to help as no Wellington boots had been provided to them. They were therefore returned to their camp. The local labourers objected to Germans getting off easy and supplied their spare boots to the Germans.[147]

Additional complaints that PoW were better dressed than the civilian population may have been true. Prisoners were provided with free uniforms, whereas the public had to make judicious use of limited clothing coupons, or 'make do and mend'.

A 'myth' persisted among the strictly rationed public that PoW were over-generously fed. One Bedfordshire man stated, 'The German PoW had egg and bacon for breakfast; we were lucky if we got an egg once a week. We had egg powder and rationing.'[148] The diet for Italians was initially the same as provided for the armed forces, but was amended to suit Italian tastes and to ensure that sufficient calories were provided for those engaged in hard manual labour. It was observed that the Italians had tinned pork and beans while the farm workers had to content themselves with bread and cheese.[149] Those billeted upon farms, however, came within the civilian rationing scheme and ate the same diet as the other farm residents. Only camps provided tinned meals, suggesting that the myth of better food has some substance.

The advent of billeting PoW on farms was generally welcomed by the farmers. Not that they always welcomed the Italians themselves, but they saw the practicalities – eliminating travelling time to and from camp would lengthen the working hours on the farm. Some Ducks Cross PoW travelled 60 miles each day, commuting to and from farms. In another attempt to reduce travelling time, bicycles were issued to PoW, which also caused resentment among a civilian population unable to obtain them themselves. The government explanation that eliminating lorry transport conserved scarce petrol and saved time failed to placate the public. Home Intelligence Weekly Report No. 82, dated 29 April 1942, recorded, 'Amongst workers in one Region who "travel in open lorries and have to put up with it" some discontent has been reported over a Press report about Italian prisoners who are stated to have "struck" because they disapproved of vehicles in which they were conveyed to work, and for whom the authorities have provided luxury coaches.'[150]

As the war progressed there was obviously rising concern at governmental level about the behaviour of PoW. This appeared to have resulted from public disquiet. A memorandum dated 4 September 1943 records, 'The Security reports from Commands have indicated considerable uneasiness amongst the public as to the inadequacy of the present control over Italian prisoners of War. This point has already been mentioned once at a previous conference, and it is proposed to raise it again.'[151] On 28 December 1944, the Home Office circulated a memorandum to all chief constables: 'As you are aware considerable publicity has been given recently to complaints about the conduct of Italian Co-operators. The War Office have found that many of these complaints, when investigated, prove to be either mere vague general statements or that even when they are specific, they are not born out by the reports received. The matter is, as you will appreciate, of concern to the Home Office from the point of view of public order, and particularly in relation to any extra duties which may be thrown on to the police; and the Home Secretary is anxious to find out how far the incidents reported in the Press and elsewhere are exceptional or exaggerated or are really representative of the general situation.'[152] The Home Office requested answers to specific questions.

The Bedfordshire Police's response has not survived, but those from the Metropolitan Police include the following generalisations: 'Behaviour on the whole good, a few complaints of molesting of women and girls and petty pilfering. One or two minor instances of being found in licensed premises, but in such cases the landlord appeared to be ignorant of the regulations. Police officers have commented that in some of the poorer districts some females, particularly young girls, are inclined to force their attention on the Italians. No outstanding instances of public feeling against these men have been brought to notice.'[153] From this there appears to be little substance to the government's fears, and little difference between the Italian PoW and the common man.

In an undated 'leaflet of suggestion' to clergy circulated by the British Council of Churches, it was acknowledged that the hesitation felt by British clergy on various grounds might have prevented them making contact with German PoW, and how, after many years of war, they had difficulty looking on Germans as human beings.[154] The instruction to 'Love thy enemy' comes hard. The British public's attitude could be just as inscrutable. As an Irish labourer in the brickfields said: 'What we couldn't understand, looking from a colonied perspective as Irish people, was how the English people could forgive them so quickly. "Good Old Jerry." We just couldn't understand how they could be so forgiving.'[155]

The last German PoW returned home in 1949. As peace would not be officially declared until 9 July 1951, they had been legitimately detained according to the Geneva Convention, but this does not mean that the British people felt it had been correct to do so. Harold Nicholson MP recorded in 1947, 'We have no right to use this slave labour and I feel ashamed'. Few farmers agreed with him and the public did not query who produced their food during times of scarcity.[156]

CHAPTER 6

Conclusions

Adverse comment made during the war indicates that the PoW obviously did not conform to perception held today, so why does the myth of the good Italian prisoner and bad German persist? Basically, anyone today who wishes to ascertain what a PoW was like will be faced with the same stereotype that was formed during the war. But are the factors, identified earlier, that led to a preconception of how an Italian and German PoW would behave, still valid after Second World War contemporary records are scrutinised?

The conclusion I drew from my original research was that the reality of Italian PoW life did not match present-day perceptions and memories. Richard Moore-Cooper correctly assessed that, 'Dressed in their chocolate and green prisoner of war battledress (itself a demeaning symbol of subjection), separated from their loved ones, and obliged to work in miserable conditions in the dreary winter climate of Britain, these men were unlikely to give their all.'[157]

The Italian could not have matched expectations that were erroneously based. They were a cross-section of the Italian population and therefore were never going to conform to a single stereotype. The vagaries of location and employment and a diverse British population affected everyone's outlook of them, and the development of relations between the British and the Italians. What remains, remembered for posterity, in Britain, is a distilled essence of the ideal Italian PoW.

The post-war stereotypical Italian PoW is not identical to that of 1943. I have shown that there appears to be additional information, recorded in the 1940s' contemporary records, that shows that the current perceived stereotype does not reflect the true nature of the Italian PoW. Both the 1943 and post-war stereotypes are flawed. Amedeo was an extreme case and so, at the other extreme, is the stereotypical Italian portrayed today. Somewhere between the two is the true man.

Attitudes towards Germans also changed from an image of a Nazi baby-killer to the recognition that everybody is somebody else's child. The 'one size fits all' stereotype of Italians or Germans patently does not apply. The official press stereotype existed, but once the British people had met PoW at close quarters the preconceived stereotype broke down. This is not to deny that evil men did evil things within the Nazi sphere of influence. It is just very unlikely that any of those men became PoW in Britain, and any that did were unlikely to have disclosed their true feelings to their captors.

Why, then, was the information presented here not used previously to alter the stereotype? In my opinion, this has not occurred because there has been no reason for the perception to be challenged or re-evaluated, as little research has been undertaken to identify and assess any alternative possibilities. The result of this is that the material has not been widely available to the public, giving them no opportunity for reconsideration. The same factors, which influenced our grandparents, still influence us today, albeit without the racist overtones. Post-war television continues to perpetuate the stereotype by showing 'repeats' of the wartime propaganda movies. 'For a particular generation that was too young to remember the Second World War, or for those who were born in the decade or so after it, moving pictures provided direct access to the past – Churchill was the hero; Hitler the villain. The Italians were cowards; the Japanese inexplicable and cruel; Dunkirk was a victory, and Dresden was necessary.'[158] Television still reinforces these myths by introducing the current generation to characters such as Bertolli, the Italian officer, and the Gestapo officer, Herr Flick, in *'Allo 'Allo!*

The restricted availability and the quality of official records has also contributed to the lack of change. Many of the original official records have not been open for inspection until recently. The wartime PoW personnel files kept upon prisoners are no longer available for research in this country. They were all returned to Germany and Italy to allow those countries to calculate pensions, in accordance with European Economic Community law.

Little written evidence of the adult wartime population has survived, or it was never recorded. The absence of large-scale correspondence from farmers to the press may not have been because they did not care, but because they were too busy to put pen to paper.

The failure to find records of the army's rank-and-file perceptions toward the Italian soldier does not indicate an absence of feeling. After the First World War, post-war autobiographies tend to have been written by officers, as were most surviving war diaries and other official documents. The 'other ranks' voice has not been recorded and is not heard today. The educational level and intelligence within the ranks of the Pioneer Corps' guards was, like their fitness, less than that of the field force units. This, together with the potential stigma of not being major contributors to victory, might also account for a lack of Pioneer Corps' personal memoirs.

In addition, very few PoW who came to this country left a written record. British researchers have not contacted those who returned home. Despite attempts to do so I have failed to locate a single Italian ex-PoW willing to give their version of events. Their recollections are lost to us and surviving evidence is therefore unavoidably biased in favour of British recollections. Memoirs have been written in German and Italian, but obtaining translations of these has been beyond my means.

Even when contemporary written records have survived, can they be trusted? The most cursory examination of oral and written reminiscences exposes a rich seam of affection and sentiment towards the PoW who worked on farms. Disparity between the public and private memories is understandable, but also deceptive. Those in daily contact with the prisoners became familiar with the men. In some cases, people described the prisoners as family. 'I think Italians loved us because we were as close to them as family,' is a feeling often repeated in many forms by interviewees. The association of prisoners as family members can signal that the recollections of some interviewees might well be tainted with nostalgia. This has been found to be the case with former prisoners who have returned to Australia. 'When interviewed all stated they encountered no prejudice or antagonism after returning to Australia. Only a naïve person would believe that all antagonism towards foreigners had mysteriously evaporated once the war ended.'[159]

The collection and recording of oral evidence has only been undertaken for the past twenty or so years. Generally the memories of the older generations have not been recorded. Most oral records have come from those who were children during the war, but again I am not totally confident in their accuracy. Memories play tricks. Summerfield and Peniston-Bird note that 'oral history provides evidence of experiences of which little or no trace exists in more conventional historical archives ... and demonstrates that such sources often give partial accounts that ignore or misrepresent developments that ran counter to official policy'. They also note that for various reasons the memory recall may not be accurate.[160] During the inquests, both Sidney and John Shelton admitted firing at Amedeo, but when I interviewed John, he denied his father had fired at all. The autopsy had revealed gunshot wounds to three places, so multiple shots had been fired either by John or his father, Sydney. John's recollection may be considered inaccurate after so long a period. Second World War oral history was recorded for the BBC research project 'People's War'.[161] A search of online transcripts reveals repeated threads of positive memories relating to Italian PoW in the UK. The age group of these subscribers are, bar one, those who were children when they had contact with the Italians. There are recollections that their parents disliked the PoW, but few mention negative aspects of prisoner contact with themselves, apart from one child who recalls the Pertenhall shooting.[162] He records Sidney Shelton supporting John in the bedroom. '[He] put a magazine in the Sten gun and sprayed it underneath [the bed], there was blood and guts all over the ceiling and everywhere.' A highly emotive description for someone who was not there! Children have selective memory and some remember only the happy things, perhaps especially friendly Italians. Also children may have been unaware of the darker side of wartime life, having been protected from it by adults. Today, therefore, they are unable to provide evidence; it went to the grave with the generations before them. John Shelton, when interviewed, said he was unable to recall shooting 'too far back. I remember him going to this door and I followed him ... I went and I don't remember all the shooting. He shot at me and I shot at him. And he missed and I hit.' The incident reappeared in print in 1998[163] under the heading 'What life was really like in Dad's Army...' The article highlights John Shelton's thought that Amedeo had fallen out with Private Hands over the WLA nearby, and that Amedeo was said to be 'a cheerful, charming young man and an excellent pianist'. Private Hands and his family do not get a mention from the author of the article. The reporting is balanced in favour of Amedeo and John Shelton's actions in defending himself. Only one book, *A Taste of Freedom*, recounts the deaths of Private Hands and Antonio Amedeo. It devotes a chapter to the tale.[164] Compared with evidence found elsewhere, the story is over-embellished and inaccurate. The author obviously based his piece on the *Bedfordshire Times* article, but detail is possibly fabricated.[165] John Shelton is the only person to mention Amedeo as a pianist, but this does not appear in this book, indicating that John Shelton, the only known surviving witness, may not have participated in the book's writing.

The image of the stereotypical Italian was not formulated by my generation. It already existed as the Second World War began and was enhanced and perpetuated by subsequent generations. The British treated their German and Italian prisoners very differently. Whether this was the result of pre-existing cultural preconceptions of their enemies, or based on experience during the war, there was undoubtedly a collective view that saw 'the Germans as ideologically committed and ruthless opponents who had to be treated with the utmost caution, but the Italians as basically honest and friendly people who had been led astray by Mussolini's fascism, but were nevertheless capable of redemption'.[166]

The nature of the relationship between Britain and Italy changed during the post-war period. Italy became a co-belligerent of the Allies in 1943, instead of an enemy. Italians were not treated as a defeated foe, subjected to humiliation, war-crimes trials or punishment. Instead, Italy was given preferential treatment and the indiscretions of the Mussolini years was glossed over. Perhaps historians and the public alike have been happy to let sleeping dogs lie and accept the positive, but flawed, stereotype of Italian PoW for the betterment of post-war international relations. While letting readers draw their own conclusions about the Germans, I recognise that many consider us all as Europeans today and as such we should work together. In some ways the relationships formed between the British and their PoW probably laid the foundations of post-war Europe.

The British public has never been presented with the full facts concerning the treatment of PoW in Britain. Until they are, they will continue to believe a myth founded upon inaccurate information and propaganda, reinforced by inaccuracies and supported by failing memories. However, it is better to remember with affection rather than with resentment.

Treatment of Prisoners on Farms

Transcripts of forms P.W.1, P.W.2 and P.W.3; these provide detailed instructions on how Italian PoW were to be dealt with by farmers.

DRAFT LEAFLET P.W.1, JANUARY 1942

Ministry of Agriculture and Fisheries.
Scheme for placing Italian prisoners of War to live and work on farms.
Conditions of Employment.

NOTICE TO FARMERS.

If an Italian prisoner is placed to "live" on your farm, you will be required to comply with the following conditions:-

1. Board and Lodging. You will be required to provide the prisoner with suitable lodging quarters and full board. The prisoner may either live with you or with one of your employees, or he may be accommodated in a suitable farm building (e.g. barn or outbuilding) provided the premises are healthy, warm and comfortable. You will have to supply straw to fill pallisasses, artificial light, heating, crockery, facilities for washing, baths etc.
2. A prisoner who lives and works on your farm must be provided with three meals a day on the same scale as an ordinary farm labourer who lives in. The prisoner will come under the civil rationing scheme.
3. Clothing. Clothing, including underwear and footwear, for the prisoners will be supplied by the Military Authorities. You will only be expected to supply the prisoner with special working kit (e.g. rubber boots).

4. Security Conditions. You will be responsible for the safe custody of prisoners who live and work on your farm.

5. You will be required to see that the following rules are obeyed:-
(a) Prisoners must not leave you land on weekdays except to attend religious services, for which special arrangements will be made by the Military Authorities.
(b) On Sundays, prisoners may be permitted to go freely up to a mile or thereabouts from your farm. They may not, however, go to any villages or towns or enter any shops or houses other than your house.
(c) Prisoners must not remain or go out of doors during the hours of blackout. (This condition may be waived in individual cases in the morning where it is necessary for a prisoner to attend to farm duties such as milking before daylight).
(d) Prisoners must not receive money or gifts.
(e) Prisoners must not send letters except through the Prisoner of War camp from which they were transferred to your farm.
(f) Prisoners must not fraternise with members of the public.

6. You must report any cases of bad conduct ~~or breach of the conditions of parole~~ [pencilled through in original draft] unsatisfactory work of any prisoner living with you to the Commandant of the Camp from which the prisoner was transferred.

7. Prisoners placed on individual farms will be kept under observation by the Military Authorities who will visit the farms concerned regularly. You will be required to allow the responsible Military Authorities to visit the prisoner employed by you and inspect the accommodation in which he is living.

8. Escape of Prisoners. In the event of the escape of the prisoner living and working on your farm you should report the fact at once, either in person or by telephone, to the local police and also to the Commandant of the Camp from which you received the prisoner. You must not use firearms to prevent the escape of a prisoner. You should use only sufficient violence to restrain the prisoner and then notify the local police and the Commandant of the Camp of the attempted escape.

9. Arrangements for work. Prisoners placed in individual employment with farmers are available for any find of ordinary farm work. You should see that the prisoner is kept fully employed on agricultural work from the day you accept him.

10. Hours of work. A prisoner is entitled to one rest day in each week, preferably Sunday, on which he must not be required to work. Apart from this, the daily hours of work of prisoners placed on individual

farms should not exceed those of other agricultural workers on your farm.

11. Wages and Lodging Allowance. For the services of any prisoners living and working on your farm you will be required to pay at the rate of 40/- per week for the first three months of service and thereafter at 48/- per week. Time in excess of the normal working week (as laid down by your County Wages Committee) will be charged at 1/- an hour for the first three months and 1/3d an hour thereafter.

12. The allowance to be made to you for Board and Lodging for prisoners living and working on your farm will be 21/- per prisoner per week.

13. No payment of wages or overtime should be made by you to the prisoner.

14. You must keep a careful record of the number of hours worked by the prisoner, and forward this each week to your County War Agricultural Executive Committee together with the not weekly payment (including overtime) due for the services of the prisoner after the deduction of the Board and Lodging allowance.

15. Termination of arrangements to employ prisoners. The arrangements between you and your County War Agricultural Committee for the employment of prisoners to live on your farm may be terminated by giving one week's clear notice on either side.

16. Penalties. Failure to comply with any of these conditions will involve the withdrawal of any prisoners placed with you. Any prisoners who break their conditions of parole [pencilled through in original draft] will be returned to the Camp.

DRAFT LEAFLET P.W.2, JANUARY 1942

Ministry of Agriculture and Fisheries.
Scheme for transfer of selected Prisoners of War to agricultural hutment hostels.
Conditions of Employment.

NOTICE TO FARMERS.

Farmers who wish to have the service of prisoners accommodated in the Ministry's hutment hostels will be required to comply with the following requirements.

1. Collection of prisoners from Hostels. Unless your farm is within walking distance of the hostel (3 miles) you or your representative will be required to fetch any prisoner allocated to work on your farm at the appointed hour each morning and to see that the prisoner is returned to the hostel before blackout.
2. From the time you accept the prisoner in the morning until you return him to the hostel at the end of the day you will be responsible for his safe custody.
3. Transport of prisoners to and from the hostel. Prisoners allocated to work on farms may be permitted to walk up to three miles in each direction. For greater distances you will be expected to fetch the prisoners allocated to you in one of your vehicles at your own expense.
4. Security Conditions. You will be required to see that any hostel prisoners who work on your farm:-
    (a) Do not leave your land during the working day.
    (b) Do not go to any villages or towns or any shops or houses other than your own house.
    (c) Do not receive any gifts or money.
    (d) Do not send letters except through the hutment hostel to which they are attached.
    (e) Do not fraternise with members of the public.
5. You must report any case of bad conduct or breach of the conditions set out in paragraph 4 above or unsatisfactory work of any prisoner working for you to the NCO in charge of the hostel to which the prisoner is attached (The address and telephone number of the hostel are given at the foot of this notice).
6. Hostel prisoners working on individual farms will be kept under

observation by the Military Authorities who will visit the farm from time to time for this purpose. You will be required to allow the Military Authorities to see the prisoners.

7. Clothing and food. Ordinary clothing for the prisoners working from hostels will be provided by the Military Authorities. You will be expected to supply any special working kit (e.g. rubber boots).

8. Prisoners working from hostels will be provided with their normal rations, including a haversack lunch, by the Military Authorities. It will not be necessary for you to provide the prisoner with food but only hot liquid refreshment (i.e. cocoa, coffee or soup) during the day and also, if necessary, with facilities for cooking a mid-day meal.

9. Escape of Prisoners. If a prisoner escapes while you are responsible for him, you must report the fact at once to the local police and also to the NCO of the hostel. You should not use firearms to prevent the escape of a prisoner. You should use only sufficient violence to restrain them and then notify the local police and the military guard at the hostel of the attempted escape.

10. Wages. For the services of any hostel prisoner allocated to work on your farm you will be required to pay the rate of 1/- per hour for the first 8 hours and 1/3d per hour for hours in excess of 8 per day. No charge will be made for time taken in conveying the prisoners to and from the hostel or for time (normally ½ hour) occupied for the mid-day meal.

11. A time sheet will be provided at the hostel on which you must enter the times actually worked by the prisoner. The completed time sheet for each week must be handed in or sent in to the Committee, together with the net payment due, according to the arrangements that will be notified to you by the Committee. No payment should be made by you to the prisoner.

12. You will be expected to employ any prisoner allocated to you regularly, on wet days as well as fine. If you wish to terminate the arrangements to employ a hostel prisoner, you must give at least 24 hours notice to the Committee's representative.

13. Penalties. Failure to comply with any of these conditions will involve the withdrawal of any hostel prisoners allocated to you. Any prisoners who break their conditions of parole [pencilled through in original draft] will be returned to the Camp from which they were transferred to the hostel.

DRAFT FORM P.W.3, JANUARY 1942

Application for the employment of Italian Prisoners of War to live and work on farms.

Part 1

(1) Particulars of Employer:

> Name:
> Nationality:
> Postal address of Farm:

(2) Number of prisoners required.

(3) Will you employ the prisoner(s) regularly?

(4) Give brief particulars of work on which it is intended to employ the prisoners.

(5) State the arrangements you propose to make for the accommodation of the prisoners.

I have read leaflet PoW/1 and agree to comply with the conditions set out therein.

> Signed . . . .
> (Name of Farmer)

> Date 1942

Part 2

(To be completed by County War Agricultural Executive Committee). Report and recommendation of the Committee.

If the Committee are satisfied (a) that the applicant is suitable and (b) that the labour is needed, the word 'Approved' will be sufficient. If not, reasons should be stated briefly.

War Establishment

Specimen War Establishment as at 25 July 1945[167]

V/1099/2. Italian Prisoner of War Working Camp.
(Over 1,250 prisoners of war, including attached Germans)

(i) Personnel.

Details	Officers	Warrant Officers	Serjeants	Corporals	Lance-corporals	Privates	Total
Commandant (Lt-Col.)	1						1
Ass Commandant (Major)	1						1
Adjutant	1						1
Quarter-master	1						1
Company officer (Captain, for accounts (a))	1						1
Interpreters (Subalterns, one may be a Staff-Serjeant (b))	2						2
RQMS		1					1
Provost serjeant			1				1
Police duties (c)				1	6	10	17
Escorts			1		2	9	12
Duty NCO (d)			1				1
Clerks (e)			1	1	1	4	7
Q duties				1	1		2

Details	Officers	Warrant Officers	Serjeants	Corporals	Lance-corporals	Privates	Total
Storeman						1	1
NCO for ration & postal duties				1			1
General dutyman					1		1
Drivers, IC, RASC						2	2
TOTAL, ALL RANKS	7	1	4	4	11	26	53
Attached							
ACC – cooks for other rank's meals				1			1
Total, working in camp Italian PoW	7	1	4	5	11	26	54

(ii) Transport.

Bicycles, GS. For each attached hostel	1
Motorcycles, solo	2
Car, 4x2, light utility	1
Truck, 15-cwt, 4x4 (f)	1

(a) (i) One additional company officer (subaltern) is authorised for general duties when the number of attached hostels exceeds 3, or the number of billeted prisoners of war exceeds 50.
(ii) In addition a further company officer (subaltern) will be allowed when the number of attached hostels exceeds 6, or the number of billeted prisoners of war exceeds 150.

(b) Twenty per cent of the total officer interpreters employed in this type of unit may be captains in camps where responsibilities warrant such ranks.

(c) The following will be allowed in addition for each attached working hostel:

Detail	Warrant Officer class 2	Staff-serjeant	Serjeant	Lance-serjeant	Corporal	Lance-corporals
Italian co-operator hostel						
1 – 150 Italians			1			
151– 200 Italians			1		1	
201– 300 Italians		1		1		
Over 300 Italians	1			1		
Italian non-co-operator hostels						
1 – 100 PoW			1		1	1
101 – 200 PoW			1		1	
201 – 300 PoW		1		1		2
Over 300 PoW	1			1		2
German hostel						
1 – 75 PoW			1		1	1
76 – 200 PoW			1	1		1
201 – 300 PoW		1		1		2
Over 300 PoW	1			1		2

(d)   One additional duty NCO (corporal) is authorised for every 6 attached hostels, or part of 6 over 6.

(e)   Includes 2 clerks for 750 accounts each. An additional accounts clerk is authorised for each additional 750 prisoner of war accounts, or part of 750, over 1,500.

(f)   (i) One additional truck, 15-cwt, 4x4, GS, or lorry, 3-ton, at the discretion of the G.O.C.-IN-C., will be allowed when the number of attached hostels exceeds 3, or the number of billeted Italians exceeds 50.
(ii) In addition, a further truck, 15-cwt, 4x4, GS, will be allowed when the number of attached hostels exceeds 6, or the number of billeted Italians exceeds 150.
(iii) In addition, a further car, 4x2, light utility, will be allowed, at the discretion of the G.O.C.-IN-C., will be allowed when the number of attached hostels exceeds 9, or the number of billeted Italians exceeds 300.
(iv) Drivers for these additional vehicles will be provided from the Italian Co-operators.

Notes.

1. Officers will be of a medical category lower than 'A' and other ranks will be of a medical category lower than 'A1' if available.

2. The following duties will be performed by prisoners of war:-

Cooks for:-

Officers' mess	1
Serjeants' mess	1
Rank and file mess	3
Batmen	3
Orderly for officers' mess	1
Sanitary dutyman	1

3. Italian Co-operators may be employed as below for Italian Co-operators in hostels and billets:-

Senior Warrant Officer	1
Clerk	1 for every 300 or part thereof.
Cooks and general dutymen (per hostel)	3 for every 100 or part thereof.
Shoemakers, tailors and barbers	1 of each per 250 or part thereof.
Company staff (per company of 250)	1
Serjeant (per section of 36)	1

Report on Ducks Cross

Translation of IRCC Report by Col. John Sainsbury, December 2006
P/JPe/MH Great Britain

PRISONERS OF WAR CAMP No. 72

Visited by Mr H. de Pourtables, 8 February 1943.

Postal Address Prisoners of War Camp No. 72, Great Britain.
Capacity   750 men.
Actual strength 1 Lieutenant Doctor; 19 NCO's and 683.
                             562 live in camp;
                             50 in Ministry of Agriculture Hostel;
                             91 billeted on farms.
Nationality   Italian.
Man of Confidence   Fassi, Arturo. Iio Capo Cannoniere.
Italian Doctor   Tenente Medico Fusaroli, Loris.

General description of the Camp
This camp is the model for a series of camps, all of identical layout/
construction, put up in the second half of 1942 in order to accommodate
Italian PoW who had come to Great Britain as agricultural workers.
    We propose to give a detailed description here, to which we can refer in
subsequent reports when they are dealing with the same type of camp.
    Camp 72 is situated in open countryside at some considerable distance
from the nearest inhabited area. It dominates a vast extent of country,
lightly undulating, in a rich fertile area. The site is healthy and the climate
agreeable. The camp covers an area of about seven hectares. It is divided
into rectangles by wide concrete paths alongside which the huts are

placed. These are all of the same type, each measuring 6 metres wide by 25 metres in length. The huts are not of the old 'Nissen' type, in corrugated iron, but of modern construction in materials that are both waterproof and insulating, prefabricated and put together on site. The foundations are in cement and are sufficiently raised to stop damp getting in. The walls have plenty of windows, thereby insuring there is sufficient light and ventilation.

The camp consists of about 30 of these huts, of which 21 are used as prisoner's dormitories. Of the others 3 are used as dining halls, the rest as recreation room, sick bay, kitchens, laundries, ablutions/ latrines.

The whole camp, including a huge sports field, which is beside it, is surrounded by barbed wire. Not far away is a similar camp where the British guard force and camp administration are housed.

Accommodation

The huts are lit by electricity and each has two heating stoves. A large number have been decorated with paintings by the prisoners themselves. Each hut houses 35–40 men. The beds – double bunked pattern – are placed down each side of the room, leaving a wide space down the centre. Each man has a mattress, four blankets and pillows.

Food

The kitchens are particularly well organised and managed. In the centre a big modern stove enables a variety of menus to be prepared- roasts, grills etc., while a double row of big pots is used for boiling. The prisoners make their own Italian pasta.

On the day of the visit the menus were as follows:

Breakfast: coffee with milk, bread, margarine, jam.

Lunch: minestrone, lard, bread.

Supper: meat rissoles, minestrone, coffee, bread.

In this working camp, the main meal is served in the evening, after the prisoners have returned from the fields.

The prisoners working in he kitchen and the ration store declared themselves satisfied with the quality and quantity of the rations, which conform to the regulations. In addition, each prisoner claims 2½d per day for food–purchasing supplementary foodstuffs – cake, jam etc.

Collective punishment relating to feeding has never been imposed.

Clothing
As usual the prisoners have two sets of battledress and two of underclothes
and socks. Those working on field drainage are issued with a pair of rubber
knee boots.

Washing, etc.
Two blocks are set aside for showers and washrooms. Each has 20 sets of
hot/cold water taps for ablutions and 12 shower cubicles, with hot water
as needed. Forty WCs are available to the prisoners.
[Translator's note – it actually reads 'as much hot water as they like' –
which I doubt, having lived through fuel shortages]

Medical and hygiene
A double hut is set aside as a medical centre, comprising several rooms
which are specially heated and have comfortable furniture. One room,
with waiting room, is reserved for 'visits to the doctor'. There, in order,
there are a treatment room, a dental surgery, two sick rooms, washing
facilities and Italian MO's quarters. Besides the Doctor, 7 Italian medical
orderlies look after the sick. There were only two sick on the day of the
visit- one bronchitis, one ill with a temperature- neither serious. The state
of health of the prisoners in 72 Camp is remarkably good if one bears
in mind the fact that only two out of 703 were in sick quarters. Four
prisoners were undergoing treatment in the hospital in the neighbouring
town – one under observation for TB and the others with illnesses that
were not serious – bronchitis, jaundice, piles.

Finance
All prisoners who are qualified agricultural workers receive 1s a day, unskilled
labourers 6d. They are paid in tokens, or if prisoners prefer, credited to
their accounts. As a result most prisoners have some savings. Total deposits
sometimes reach a considerable sum (as much as £600–£800). This situation
does often lead to discontent, with the prisoners wanting to buy things which
are relatively costly, such as gramophones, musical instruments, leather
suitcases etc., which are rather difficult to find in this present day market.
Apart from this, no representations were made relating to money matters.

Work
All the prisoners are engaged in agricultural work. The daily timetable is
arranged to fit with the length of daylight hours. In Winter work will not
last more than 6–7 hours, while in Summer it can go on for as long as 11
hours. Pay is normally based on an 8 hour day. When the prisoners have to
do overtime it is paid at a rate of two cigarettes per hour.

The majority of prisoners live in camp and are taken by lorry every morning to their workplace (as much as 30 km away), and brought back in the evening. Fifty prisoners live in a hostel, i.e., a place specially set up by the Ministry of Agriculture for the purpose. Further, 91 men are distributed in small groups of 3–12 with farmers who provide food and lodging. This system seems to function to the satisfaction of both sides – the prisoners appreciate the advantages they have and the farmers generally praise their work.

Canteen
The camp canteen is well provided with all sorts of things, such as toilet requisites, matches, writing materials, cakes and cigarettes. Receipts amount to about £500 per month. The result is considerable benefit to the camp- further increasing available funds.

As previously, the prisoners receive a free issue of 35 cigarettes per week.

Leisure facilities, spiritual and intellectual needs
In view of the hard work done by the prisoners, and the small amount of free time they have, sports requirements are few. However, a football pitch has been set up in the camp, which the prisoners use sometimes on Sundays.

The Italian MO is allowed on parole to go for walks outside the camp.

The library in this camp, which opened recently, is almost non-existent. Books in Italian cannot be found in England. The visiting team note that any books the Italian Red Cross are able to send would be welcome.

The prisoners have constructed a small theatre in the recreation room and are asking for musical instruments. No study-classes have been held to date. Nevertheless a number of prisoners who are illiterate want to receive primary education.

The prisoners have obtained a radio set. It is being installed.

No Italian priest is a prisoner in the camp, however Mass is celebrated every Sunday by an English priest who comes from the nearest town.

Correspondence
The prisoners are allowed to write one letter and one card each week and regularly receive mail from Italy. It takes about five weeks for the mail to reach camp. Italian Red Cross parcels are rare, but on the other hand those sent by their families are more numerous, although according to the prisoners some are lost on the way.

Complaints and requests
No complaints have been brought to the notice of the visiting team. Requests, to, are few in number and are mainly concerned with despatch of books and musical instruments.

Deaths
There has been one death, due to an accident at work – that of Eugenio Bracco, who was crushed by a lorry. This accident, which took place in November, was notified at the time.

Conclusion
This camp gives an excellent impression. The state of health of the prisoners is exceptionally good, and morale also. The prisoners, and especially those living on farms, say that they are satisfied with their treatment from both material and morale standpoints.

APPENDIX 4

Camp Maintenance

Abstract from War Office Administrative Instructions Relating to PoW Camp Maintenance Staff, 1 June 1944[168]

In order to maintain the camp facilities and provide the requisite catering and living standards a common standard was laid down. From a camp, 7 per cent of the total PoW strength were authorised to be engaged upon internal employments.

These figures are based upon an average camp strength as follows:-

In camp	750
In 3 Hostels	210
In Billets	50
Total	1,010

PoW not engaged in external work were utilised as follows:-

Cooks & assistants	22
Hut orderlies	12
Dining Room orderlies	3
Ablution/latrine orderlies	2
Canteen staff	1 (a)
Teachers	2
Clerks for Accounts Officer	2
Clerks for Interpreter	1
Clerks for Camp Leader	1
Shoemakers	4 (b)(c)
Tailors	3 (c)
Barbers	3 (c)

Sewage Disposal	2 (c)(d)
2 cooks at each Hostel	6
2 orderlies at each Hostel	6
Total	70

(a) Non-working NCO
(b) Includes repair of rubber boots with vulcaniser
(c) Includes work for British troops
(d) Where necessary

The following PoW could be employed in addition to the 7 per cent:

(1) In the compound:-
    (i) Camp Leader & Deputy
    (ii) Protected personnel
    (iii) Special cases e.g. for bucket latrine for which WO authority must be obtained
    (iv) English-speaking PoW posted to camp by WO as interpreters

Note:- Where there are co-operators in hostels or billets, tailors, shoemakers, barbers and medical orderlies must also be co-operators.

(2) In the British Lines (allowed by War Establishment):-
    (i) 3 Batmen
    (ii) 5 Cooks
    (iii) 1 Officer's Mess Orderly
    (iv) 1 Sanitary dutyman

Note:- Cookhouse fatigues in the British Cookhouse will be performed by PoW on light duties or undergoing detention.

(3) A camp maintenance gang (carefully selected as to their suitability):-
    (i) 2 Carpenters
    (ii) 1 Bricklayer
    (iii) 1 Bricklayer's labourer
    (iv) 1 Plumber
    (v) 1 Plumber's mate

Note:- This maintenance gang is to be made available when required by an official of the Ministry of Works and Planning and may at other times on the request of a CRE be made available for RE works services within a radius of 30 miles from the camp. When the gang is required by neither Ministry of Works or CRE the Camp Labour Officer should be informed in order that they may be employed either on the repair of farm buildings or in ordinary agricultural work.

PoW detailed for this gang will not be transferred to other camps without reference to the War Office (P.W.1).

APPENDIX 5

Accounts of the Camps

COLMWORTH CAMP, 14/15 JULY 1945

Visit by Staff from Control Office for Germany and Austria and Foreign Office, German Section. Prisoners of War: Segregation Section. Report of Mr James Grant's visit to Colmworth Camp, Bedford, 14/15 July 1945.[169]

This is a camp with a vigorous community life. Everyone on the compound with whom I spoke, at once asked if it were not the best camp I had seen. The church was lavishly decorated in a colourful, Italianate way, the theatre also has every square inch painted by the Italians who were there, and even on the doorways of the dining-rooms appear rather humorous cartoon. Many of the blackout boards have country scenes painted, with groups of cows and other animals. There are two orchestras, one with six camp made mandolins, another with three violins, two saxophones, and accordion and a cello. I attended a very good concert and heard the choir sing excellently. I give these details, which are really outwith the purpose of my visit, but they give the tone of everything in the camp.

My visit took place on Saturday and Sunday, and so I was able to see classes, instruct and examine the teachers, etc. On Saturday afternoon and Sunday morning and afterwards, good progress had been made in the classes, where the teaching was surprisingly free from scholastic dryness, and there is a complete school running in the evenings from 8.30 to 10.30. Besides English they have history, chemistry, mathematics, Russian, French, Spanish, shorthand, business methods, book-keeping and sign-writing. One cannot help feeling in this camp that a great number of men will leave it better prepared for their future life, both technically and psychologically.

The English books in the library are too difficult for the average student of the advanced class. The Unterrichtsleiter asked if it would not be possible to have some copies of some novels for study and comment; he himself had done this at school with *The Vicar of Wakefield* and would like this one, or some work of Kipling.

The teachers in this camp are:-

Freitz WALSER (35) who learned English in the Oberrealschule, Friedenstadt, Scharzwald. Was a studienrat in Madrid for three years. Gives Spanish course, history, chemistry and mathematics in the schools, and does not go out to work daily. He has 20 advanced pupils, 25 intermediate, and two beginners courses. 80 in all. Some of these are men on the camp staff.
Tested: Beginners 90; Intermediate 89: Advanced 81

Otto HORN (39) Learned English in the Realgymnasium in Berlin, and was a bank clerk in Berlin before the war. He has two Russian groups with thirty pupils, and teaches 25 in the intermediate English section.
Tested: Beginners 80; Intermediate 78; Advanced 62

Alfred SCHMITT (19) learned English from his mother and had just passed Abitur at the Gymnasium in Ludwigshafen and wanted to study medicine at Heidelberg when he was called up. He has only eight advanced pupils at present, but this group is due for increases from some of the upper section.
Tested: Beginners 94; Intermediate 87; Advanced 85

All the classes in the school are three-quarters of an hour, and English is the only subject which gets three hours a week. Three dining rooms are set aside for teaching after the evening meals, and there are three blackboards, one of which is very good.

The Unterrichtsleiter would like some reading material for himself and for his pupils. I arranged with the Commandant that three English daily newspapers, from the officer's mess, be passed on the following day to the Unterrichtsleiter, who said that there was enough material in them to keep the pupils busy.

I left Directives 1–4, Imperative Drill, Faucett-Kaki word-list, having explained and given examples of the use to which they could be put.

DUCKS CROSS CAMP, 28/30 MARCH 1946

Visit to No. 72 GW Camp at Ducks Cross, Colmworth, Bedford, on 28/30 March 1946, by staff from Control Office for Germany and Austria and Foreign Office, German Section. Prisoners of War: Segregation Section.[170] Special Object of Visit – Progress Report

Strength	Officers 2. Other Ranks 817. Total 819.
Of which	80 in Roxton Hostel (3 m)
	35 in billets
Screening figures:	A – 344 Cards completed – All
	A/B – 15

420 Present complexion – White/grey
18 Candidates for b'field – Nil

Unscreened – 23   German or Austrian – German

Personnel:
Camp Commandant: Col. Ford, OBE   Camp Leader: St PoW Baber (B)
Interpreter: None   Deputy C/L: PoW Perschke (A)
                                                German MO: Oberst Rupp (C)
                                                Hostel Leader: Dettmar (B)
                                                Deputy: Sasymannahansen (B)

Reception
We were received with great cordiality by the Commandant and his Adjutant, Captain Ellis who is very co-operative. The Interpreter, S/Sgt Eaton only appeared for an hour and left on the last day of our visit to attend a course. He does not appear to command the confidence of British Staff.

History of Camp
There have been no changes since the last visit. An intake of 180 from US was expected on the day following our visit.

The camp leader, a regular soldier of 45, is suited by his wisdom and steadiness to his post. He is graded C in an internal screening carried out by the whites themselves in the early days of the camp because he ordered the use of the military salute to British staff and of the Nazi salute among PoW. His deputy, also a regular soldier, and the hostel leader at Roxton are sound and able men.

The MO, Oberst Rupp (C), was well spoken of by all witnesses and has a letter of recommendation from the Dame of Sark, where he was stationed before surrender. Despite the lack of evidence I consider nevertheless that he may play a part. As he enjoys the confidence of the British staff and as an MO to a number of other camps has ample opportunity of making contacts, his grading is of some importance.

The Interpreters, Knispel (A, est A+) and Hirsch (A, est A+) both excellent types, were very outspoken on the subject of repatriation. Knispel, aged 23, was brought up as a pacifist by his foster-parents and claims that he did not fire a shot in the war.

Morale

Is lower than at any camp I have visited. Living conditions are excellent and PoW are sympathetically treated by an able British staff. The prevailing mood of the camp, however, is one of indignation at the continued detention of whites. Many men were democratic before their capture and state that they have constantly been promised early repatriation. All witnesses showed strong feeling on this matter, whites of an excellent type displaying obvious resentment at our discussing re-education in the absence of any satisfactory answer to their questions about repatriation. The greatest bitterness is among some 100 men who at Colchester declared themselves openly as anti-Nazi before the end of the war in the face of 6,000 of their fellow prisoners. Interviews were difficult in this atmosphere, especially in the case of the RC padre, who was on the verge of hysteria. The following individual opinions are worth quoting:

Camp Leader: The introduction of postal service with the Russian Zone has caused discontent as PoW learn not only that reconstruction is more rapid under Russians but that prisoners are being released more quickly. Many decent men are consequently turning into Communists.

Hirsch, Interpreter (A): Promise after promise of early repatriation for anti-Nazis has been broken. Anti-British feeling is growing, especially among the group which declared itself as anti-Nazi before the capitulation at 186 [Beresford Hall Camp, near Colchester, Essex].

Knispel, Interpreter (A): We who declared ourselves at 186 hear from wireless, press and mail that others are released, while the whites are still detained. In letters from home we learn that our wives are taunted by repatriated Nazis and SS men about our continued detention.

A direct consequence of this reaction is the swing to communism mentioned in the next section.

Political Progress
The screening figures (A 45%, B 50%, C 2%, unscreened 3%) still hold good as far as B's and C's are concerned. The sense of grievance over the repatriation question has resulted, however, in some of the A's veering towards a communist, or perhaps more truly, Russophil outlook, which is accompanied by hostility towards Britain. For 45% A I should now substitute 23% A and 10% A-. Although there are 50–80 ardent convinced communists, described however as 'decent and quiet members of the camp' the pro-Russian swing has in many men no ideological basis and indicates the belief that Germany is getting a fairer deal from the Russians than from Britain.

There are no self-confessed Nazis. Some of the men who used to profess Nazi views are now to be found among the communists.

Youth
No special problems.

Re-educational Activities
The material facilities for re-education are excellent and there is adequate talent. There are, however, many pre-1933 democrats who consider that re-education is preaching to the converted as far as a great part of the camp is concerned and who are interested only in the date of their repatriation. The Study Organiser, Waltzer (A) is able and efficient. The principal part in re-education is played by Dr Moehrlein (B, est A). The Commandant believes on strength of remarks by his Batman that he is a communist, but although he is well to the left all witnesses maintained that this was not the case. The camp has eight men at Wilton Park, but they are not expected by camp opinion to contribute much to re-education. Four of them are reputed to be communists. Schnirpel (B) was appointed Study Leader at Roxton Hostel.

P.I.D. Activities
Wochenpost & Ausblick: see Appendix B. [missing from file.]

Newspapers: British newspapers are adequate. The 'Basler Nachrichten' is received from Geneva and is censored by S/Sgt Seaton.

Library: Adequate; efficiently run by Walzer.

Lectures: Interest has fallen off and PoW are now only willing to attend lectures if they think the lecturer can tell them something about the date of repatriation or, failing that, something about present conditions in

Germany. Only 20 men turned up for Dr Friedman's lecture last week—only partly because this coincided with a performance in the camp theatre.

Both British staff and the Germans expressed their dissatisfaction at the attitude of the lecturer, who, it is said, informed PoW that he had no interest in their questions. There were also complaints that the lecturers cover the same ground as has already been very efficiently covered by their own lecturer, Dr Moehrlein.

Discussion Groups: There were 200 applications for membership of the group formed by Dr Moehrlein. Only 120 were accepted. There are other smaller groups.

Films: There is a request for films showing actual conditions in Germany and the work of reconstruction going on there. PoW quoted a recent film on Ulster's contribution to the war effort as an example of films which lacked any kind of interest for them.

Wireless: Both the main camp and the hostel have sets, but the amplifier in the latter has been out of order since November so that only a limited number of PoW can take advantage of the broadcasts. The Commandant has not been able to get repairs carried out.

Camp Magazine: This is almost entirely the work of Dr Moehrlein and, although good in itself, suffers from lack of a broader basis. It was suggested to the Study Organiser that he endeavour to form a magazine with contributions from the mass of PoW. There is a shortage of paper.

Other Camp Activities
Religion: The camp is approximately evenly divided between the Roman Catholic and Evangelical confessions. Both padres are graded 'A'. The Evangelical, Bluthartt, is a conscientious man, has a regular attendance of 40% at his services, runs religious discussion groups and holds regular classes for religious instruction. The R.C., Bettinger, is a sincere and very excitable type who, in a painful interview, became almost hysterical in expressing his disillusionment and that of his flock over British policy towards anti-Nazi PoW. Both padres stressed the difficulty they are experiencing in keeping the sense of bitterness at bay and their incapability of giving a confident answer to the increasingly frequent questions about the length of their captivity. If the bitterness which Bettinger presented to us is also displayed to his congregation no worse influence on morale could be imagined. All the available evidence, however, indicated that in his relationships with his congregation he has sufficient sense of

responsibility not to reveal his own feelings. His attitude and influence should nevertheless be watched.

Theatre: A new theatre will be completed by July. The present building can only seat 150. Production is in the hands of Partels (A/B), who knows his job. There are 22 performers who give a show each Saturday and Sunday. There are no re-educational plays.

Orchestra: A choir and sextet give regular performances.

Conclusions
All the necessary conditions for re-education are present. The camp has, however, reached the stage at which the work of re-education can be considered virtually complete and at which a serious deterioration has begun owing to the absence of any prospect of repatriation for those who, as it is considered, have proved themselves fitted to take part in the reconstruction of Germany. A statement on the repatriation question was read out and posted. The reaction to this statement should be ascertained by the next T.A., who should also check on the influence of the Catholic padre and Dr. Moerhrlein.

Recommendations
That the urgent need of an official announcement regarding the repatriation of PoW be represented to the authorities concerned
    That a lecture on present conditions in Germany be given by a lecturer.
    That plays for a cast of 10 be supplied.

DUCKS CROSS CAMP, 28 JUNE 1946

Report of visit to No. 72 Camp at Ducks Cross, Colmworth, Bedford, on 28 June 1946. Visit by Mr H. Hansen & Capt. Charles Chubb. Control Office for Germany and Austria and Foreign Office, German Section: Prisoners of War: Segregation Section.[171]

Commandant: Col. Ford, OBE   Interpreter: S/Sgt. G Paul.
Camp Leader: 394108 Stfw. Willi Baber (B+). Dep. C/L: 537562 Ofw. Fritz Reinhart.

Camp Strength: 2,367. Officers: 3, Other Ranks: 2,364

1. Analysis of Screening.
    (i) Complete Camp (including hostels and billetees)

	During this visit (inc re-screening)	Previously graded & not re-screened	Final state of gradings
A+	12	2	14
A	30	319	349
A-	nil	nil	nil
B+	99	93	192
B	323	926	1249
B-	232	27	259
C	173	81	254
C+	44	nil	44
U/K	6	nil	6
Totals	919	1448	2367

(ii) Hostels

	Farndish	Upper Dean	Cockayne Hatley	Ravensden
A+	Nil	Nil	10	1
A	Nil	Nil	8	5
A-	Nil	Nil	Nil	Nil
B+	4	12	12	8
B	25	28	162	39
B-	17	38	16	42
C	4	3	12	5
C+	Nil	Nil	Nil	Nil
U/K	1	Nil	Nil	Nil
Totals	51	81	220	100

	Milton Ernest	Potton	Highlands Farm	Harrold	Roxton
A+	Nil	1	Nil	Nil	Nil
A	3	6	36	18	23
A-	Nil	Nil	Nil	Nil	Nil
B+	Nil	42	Nil	2	2
B	10	366	42	28	52
B-	25	57	Nil	Nil	Nil
C	78	86	1	Nil	Nil
C+	35	7	Nil	Nil	Nil
U/K	1	1	Nil	Nil	Nil
Totals	152	556	79	48	77

2. Reception.

We were well received by the Commandant and his staff. The Adjutant, Capt. Ellis, was especially cooperative and afforded us every assistance. It was not possible to keep PoW in from work and neither accommodation nor meals of any kind could be provided at the camp.

3. German Camp Staff.

a) Camp Leader: 394108 Stfw. Baber, Willi (B+). Age 45. He was a regular from 1919–31, after which he started a grocery business. He joined the party in June 1933 and remained a member until the end of 1934. In 1935 he rejoined the Army as a quartermaster. He has been C/L here since Sept 1944 and has performed his duties in a most satisfactory manner. At first he was not popular as an old soldier among the anti-Nazis in the camp. He was graded B at a previous screening, but we consider that he is now a B+ and have upgraded him accordingly. The Cdt. is well satisfied with him.

b) Deputy C/L: 537562 Ofw. Reinhardt, Fritz (A). Age 34. This PoW has just been made Deputy C/L in succession to Perschke, who has taken over the Ravensden Hostel. Reinhardt is a locksmith by trade, but was called up in 1937. He has no party affiliations and was one of the leading anti-Nazis in this country and this camp. He is very reliable and completely satisfactory.

c) Organiser of Studies: 976916 Gefr. Walser, Fritz (already graded A). Age 36. He is a Studienrat by profession and received his appointment in 1936. He was in the SA 33–37 and a Pg from 1937; but he had to join a party organisation of some kind on account of his profession. Walser succeeded Dr Moerhrlein on the latter's repatriation and does his job well as far as plain education is concerned. For political re-education, however, he freely admits that he has no aptitude.

d) Medical Officers:
(i) Main camp:
B123069 C/arzt Rupp, Wilhelm (B). Age 54. Before 1935 he had a lucrative practice at Gliessen a.d. Lahn. He joined the party in 1933, but claims that after the Rohn Affair he was disillusioned and therefore decided to join the regular Army in 1934, after which he had no further association with the Party. Before he was captured he was M.O. in the Channel Islands and states that the Dame of Sark expressed her gratitude to him for his work in assisting the islanders. The Cdt. and British staff have a good opinion of him, which is shared by the British medical officers with whom he works on the repatriation boards throughout Eastern Command. Reliable whites in the camp stated that he has never shown any militaristic or political tendencies and that they also have a good opinion of him. There is no doubt that he is a first class Doctor and is very interested in his work. He has previously been graded 'C', but we have upgraded him to 'B'.

446723 U/arzt Bedarwe, Karl (A). We found that he had already been screened 'A' previously and that he is both efficient and reliable. The British staff have a good opinion of him.

(ii) Potton Hostel:
954473 O/arzt Dr. Schemann, Paul (B). Aged 53. He was in the party and NSKK from Dec 1933, but his interest lies only in his medical work.

He is a typical provincial Doctor, does his work well and is liked by the British staff.

e) Padres: A970542 Uffz. Bluthardt, Alfred (A). Aged 36. He is the Protestant padre and has no political background, and is very popular in the camp. He is both capable and sincere.

No. 631727 San O/Gefr. Bettinger, Wilhelm (A). Age 34. He is the R.C. priest and likewise has no Party affiliations. He is popular in the camp and well suited to his work. Both padres show a keen interest in the younger PoW and impartial white PoW observers state that they exercise a beneficial influence.

f) PoW Interpreters: 191319 Gefr. Gutzeit, Heinz (B). Age 24. He was a student before the war and belonged only to the N.S. Studentendund. He was not in the Hitler Youth. He is a graduate of the special YMCA teachers camp. His previous grading was 'C', but we consider that he is now a 'B' and have upgraded him accordingly.

4. Hostel Leaders.
a) Farndish: B733397 Uschn, Hans (B-). Age 26. He joined the SS Police Division in 1943. He was appointed Hostel leader as the senior ranking PoW among the draft of young SS men posted directly to this hostel before it was taken over by this camp HQ and was not changed by the Cdt. because none of the hostel had been screened. He is entirely satisfactory from the administration point of view, but now that the hostel has been screened we have advised the Cdt. to replace him with an older 'A' category PoW to give a lead with re-education.

b) Upper Dean: B574129 Usche, Hans (B-). Age 22. He is an electrician by trade and joined the Waffen SS in 1941. he became H/L as the highest ranking PoW in the draft of very young SS men posted to this hostel before it was taken over by this camp. He has been satisfactory, but his youth and inexperience make him quite useless as far as re-education is concerned and we have advised the Cdt. to replace him with an older white PoW.

c) Cockayne Hatley: A809075 Ofw. Stopel, Erich (B). He is a regular soldier, but served only in the regimental band. There were no adverse criticisms of him either from the British staff or the PoW in the hostel which contains a high number of prisoners.

d) Ravensden: 902402 Stfw. Perschke, Alfred (A). A regular soldier, already previously graded 'A' who was, until this new hostel was taken over during our visit, Deputy C/L at the main camp. He is an excellent type and is liked by the British staff and the PoW. He is cooperative and interested in re-education and has a sound knowledge of the correct psychological approach to the young and mostly disillusioned B-type of PoW under his command.

e) Milton Ernest: A970157 PoW Mueller, Walter (C). Age 31. He is a baker by trade, but was called up in 1937. We found that he had previously been graded 'A', but on asking him how he got on with his hostel, which is jet black in political colouring, we were astounded when he replied 'Very well indeed.' When questioned as to his present attitude to Nazism he replied 'I did not have a bad life under the Third Reich.' To the question 'Why did Germany lose the war?' he gave the answer 'Because of disagreement among the Service chiefs.' We have downgraded him to 'C' and the Cdt. has agreed to remove him from the hostel and replace him with a strong A+ white.

f) Potton: B74498 Ofw. Boslet, Werner (A+). He was called up in 1938 and is a well educated and very reliable type who was already graded 'A+'. He is efficient and diplomatic and has the complete confidence of the white PoW and the British staff. He was a correspondent of a small newspaper before the war. He was formerly C/L of No. 19 PoW Camp (Nov 44–Aug 45). He is interested in re-education and has been fairly successful in dealing with a recent unruly intake of black PoW from Canada. He is the right man in the right job.

g) Highland Farm: A968129 Wm. Renner, Alfred (B) He has proved entirely satisfactory to the Cdt. and there were no criticisms of him from the PoW, who are mostly white. He is a steady and capable type of man is well suited for his job.

h) Harrold: A980222 Wm. Gedies, Herbert (A). He is one of the original anti-Nazis from this camp who gave valuable assistance to the IO in sorting out the Nazis here as long ago as the end of 1944. He has also played a useful part in the re-education programme and enjoys the full confidence of the British staff and PoW alike.

i) Roxton: A968826 Fw. Dettmar, Hans (B). A steady type of individual who gets on well with the mainly white PoW in this hostel, which is the oldest satellite camp on the strength of this unit and is regarded by the British staff as a model hostel. He is reliable and suited for the job.

5. Political Complexion
The political state of this camp is highly complex and in view of the varying circumstances in the nine hostels it is necessary to deal with them separately.

(a) Main camp: This camp was one of the earliest anti-Nazi camps in Great Britain and still contains a large number of whites who have been here since the end of 1944. These men are indignant at their long detention in captivity in spite of their anti-Nazi sentiment, and the alleged fact that Nazis have already been released and hold good positions in Germany. They no longer have the missionary spirit for re-education and in spite of the fact that this camp has this year received a large number of fresh intakes from Belgium, Canada and the USA, all of them are badly in need of re-education, the prevailing spirit among the old white PoW is one of apathy. The all-pervading depression and bitterness has resulted in a complete lack of interest and produced a Russophile state of mind among 10–15 per cent of them.

The PoW from the USA are also suffering from a feeling of indignation at the failure to implement the promise made in America that they would be home in three weeks. They hold the British responsible now for their detention. Their political complexion is grey/black. The blacks are largely former members of the Afrika Corps who were captured in 1943, whilst the greys are men who have been superficially influenced by the American equivalent of re-education, but generally state that they have been away from Germany too long to have any opinion. There are also complaints that the rations they receive in this country are insufficient.

The Canadian drafts contained many PoW who have been prisoners from 4 to nearly 7 years and some of them still have in their minds the picture of Germany as it was in 1939 and 1940. Such types are mainly very black. The greys are PoW who were never ardent Nazis, but have been so long in captivity that they seem to be incapable of forming any opinion and indeed lack the necessary interest to take part in any educational or re-educational activities.

The various recent drafts from Belgium, and especially those from camp 22/24 at Jabeccy arrived in a poor physical condition and a number of undernourished PoW are still resting in the camp and receiving supplementary rations to fit them for work again. The bad treatment they received is reflected in their mental and political outlook and although they are not, in the main, convinced Nazis, at the same time they are most difficult to grade because they are not at present too conscious of their recent misfortunes and are too dazed and apathetic to show any interest in politics or even to express any opinion about anything. Some of the stronger types still state, however, that life in concentration camps could not have been very much worse than what they found in Belgium. Others stated that they could not believe in the sincerity of our anti-militarism, since in Belgium the worst types of diehard militarist Germans were appointed to the camp leadership and staff, and the treatment they meted out to their fellow PoW was even more militaristic than in the German army. Although the indignation is mainly directed against the German staff, who are alleged also to have purloined rations, they argue that it is difficult to understand why such obvious militarists and 'thugs' should have been supported and even encouraged by the Cdt.

All these PoW expressed their gratitude for the sense of freedom and good treatment since they have been in England and we feel that after their rehabilitation they will in course of time become good material for re-education.

There is, in our opinion, no real Communist group in this camp, although, for the reason already given, some of the older anti-Nazis are forming the opinion that German PoW are getting a better deal from the Russians. At the same time, it is of interest that just as many of them, whose homes are in the Russian Zone, have asked whether they may be permitted to return on repatriation to the British Zone as they state they have no wish to go back to the Russian occupied areas of Germany. During our visit there was great excitement in the camp at the news that 46 prisoners are to be repatriated to the British Zone. These men are all original anti-Nazis from the early days of this camp and their return should help to raise the extremely low morale of heir fellow whites. Before we left the camp, however, we were informed by one of the prisoners that the Russians had announced that they intend to release over 1,000,000 German PoW before the end of this year. This was alleged to have been heard over the wireless and had led to intense speculation in the camp. To sum up the position of the old whites in this camp, it is clear that their nervous irritation at their long detention has produced a state of mind in which they have to find a scapegoat and be anti-something or simply relapse into general apathy. The latter category are likely to be encouraged by the new scheme of repatriation from England. The former, who are about 10–15% form a see-saw group whose opinions are likely to be affected by news of repatriation schemes and general living conditions and prospects from the Russian or Western Zones of Germany. At present their scapegoat is this country. Future developments in this country will depend largely on the provision of an effective PoW Director of Re-education. The prisoner formerly responsible for re-educational work in this camp (Dr Moehrlein) has been repatriated, and there is no one here who is suitable to replace him. The PoW in the main camp who have been to Wilton Park (Sich, Pionetek, Roehrs, Bambach and Heare) have a beneficial but restricted influence in their daily contacts, but are by no means suited for the post. There is great need for re-education owing to the presence of so many blacks and greys from overseas. Material conditions in the camp are excellent, and the Cdt has a great interest in, and a sound understanding of PoW psychology. All that is lacking is a sound and outstanding PoW re-educator to organise and co-ordinate re-educational activity in the main camp and its numerous hostels.

(b) Hostels:

a. Farndish: The PoW arrived early in Mast last from Belgium, and the hostel is composed entirely of young Waffen SS men who were forcibly directed to that unit in 1943-44-45. They are all under 25 years of age. They created a very good impression and are keen to learn anything and everything about democracy. They are ready for the full impact of re-education, but at present there is nothing at all apart from Wochenpost. There are no books or English papers and they badly need grammars to learn English.

b. Upper Dean: The PoW also arrived in may from Belgium and their ages range from 18–25. They were called up forcibly 1943–44–45. They are in just as receptive frame of mind as their fellow prisoners at Farndish hostel, since, in common with them, they saw with their own eyes the final collapse of Nazism in Germany. They are ripe for re-education. There are no books, English papers or wireless, and grammars are needed to learn English. Many PoW complained of the complete lack of news from home.

c. Cockayne Hatley: A grey/white hostel with a high percentage of outstanding 'A+' cases, mainly prisoners of the anti-Nazi movement in the camps in the USA. The latter PoW are disillusioned to find themselves in England and consider that a mistake must have been made, since ardent Nazis who left America at the same time as themselves have been repatriated to Germany. The 'A+' PoW are largely, however, from the Russian Zone. We recommended to the Cdt. that these 'A+' men be sent to the more backward hostel.

d. Potton: The complexion of this hostel was grey/white until the arrival of a Canadian intake some 3–4 months ago. Amongst the latter we found a high percentage of 'C' and 7 'C+', and the C/L stated that this Nazi nucleus is having an adverse effect upon the younger former members of his hostel. The C/L was therefore urged to organise a new re-educational programme to counteract this effect. Most of the PoW in this hostel are living in tents.

e. Ravensden: This is an entirely new hostel filled during our visit with PoW from Belgium. It is a mixture of categories from 'A+' to 'C' and most of the men were called up forcibly to the Waffen SS in 43-44-45. Many of them state they were promised repatriation after the completion of specific tasks in Belgium and that they were even issued with release certificates by the Belgians: but that these promises certificates (which some of them still possess) were ignored in the English controlled PoW camps to which they were subsequently sent. One man complained of very bad treatment at the hands of the Dutch in Holland after the end of the war. Effective re-education is badly needed here, but the C/L is capable and very judicious and already having a good influence on them.

f. Milton Ernest: This is an extremely black hostel and there are no less than 78 'C' and 35 'C+' in a total strength of 152. The whole draft came from the U.S.A. and are mostly prisoners long in captivity, who remember only the successful days of Germany in 1939-40. A graduate of Wilton Park (Hasback, Johannes (A)) was sent from the main camp to undertake re-education: but he is completely overwhelmed by the super-Nazi atmosphere and although he is keen and intelligent he cannot be expected to have the slightest effect. He confirmed our findings and agreed that the bad blacks were wildly fanatical and dangerous types who would start to work for the re-birth of Nazism in Germany. We strongly recommend that all the 'C+' be removed as soon as possible, since nothing can be done to re-educate them in this working camp. We have also recommended to the Cdt. that as soon as this happens all the 'C' should be brought into the main camp and replaced by greys.

g. Roxton, Highland Farm, Harrold: These three hostels are comparatively long established and were filled with greys and whites from the HQ camp. They have not been affected by new intakes and are all white/grey in texture, faithfully reflecting the political texture of their white comrades in the main camp. A PID lecturer (Mr Senf) who visited Highlands Farm reported that the only topic in which PoW were interested was the date of their repatriation.

6. Re-education.
Since the last T.A. visit at the end of March the political complexion has been greatly changed by the overseas intakes. We tried wherever possible to galvanise the older members of the camp into re-education activity to cope with the solid mass of blacks and greys; but we recommend that a T.A. should visit the camp to see what progress, if any, has been made. A visit from an English inspector would also be useful and worthwhile at Farndish, Upper Dean and Ravensden hostels.

7. Recommendations.
a) That a first-class PoW graduate from Wilton Park be posted to this camp to take over the duties of Director of Re-education.

b) That all 'C+' be removed from this camp as soon as possible.

c) That as many English grammars as possible be sent and earmarked for use in Farndish, Upper Dean and Ravesden hostels.

d) That a T.A. and an English Inspector should visit the camp and new hostels.

Endnotes

1. Field, Geoffrey, 'Social Patriotism and the British Working Class: Appearance and Disappearance of a Tradition.' *International Labor and Working Class History* 42 (Fall 1992): 27. Quoted in Geoff Eley, 'Finding the People's War: Film, British Collective Memory, and World War II,' *The American Historical Review*, Vol. 106, No. 3. (Jun., 2001), pp. 818–838.
2. *Farmers Weekly*, 28 February 1941.
3. Murray, K. A. H. *History of the Second World War: United Kingdom Civil Service.* Vol. 2, Agriculture, London, HMSO 1955.
4. Calder, Angus. *The People's War.* Jonathan Cape, London, 1969.
5. Murray, K. A. H. *History of the Second World War: United Kingdom Civil Service.* Vol. 2, Agriculture, London, HMSO 1955.
6. Murray, K. A. H. *History of the Second World War: United Kingdom Civil Service.* Vol. 2, Agriculture, London, HMSO 1955.
7. Hansard, House of Commons, fifth series (1939–40).
8. TNA. ADM1/11640.
9. TNA. WO32/9904.
   Department of Transport – 4,000.
   Director of Fortifications & Works [Army] – 2,000 on forestry work.
   Director if Supply & Transport [Army] – 600 in Royal Army Service Corps depots.
   Director of Ordnance Services [Army] – 2,175 in Ordnance works.
   Ministry of Agriculture – 1,000.
   Ministry of Supply – (Forestry) – number unspecified, dependent upon the security of small group working.
10. TNA. WO32/9904.

11.   TNA. CAB114/25.

12.   TNA. CAB114/25.

13   TNA. MAF47/54.

14.   TNA. FO939/357.

15.   Montgomery, J. K., 'The Maintenance of the Agricultural Labour Supply in England & Wales during the War,' *International Review of Agriculture*, Rome, 1922. (Originally published in the International Review of Agricultural Economics). Reviewed *The Economic Journal*, Vol. 33, No. 130 (June 1923), pp 232–234.

16.   TNA. 25/11/41. Minute 40A relating to introduction of Hostel scheme.

17.   TNA. WO166/6018.

18.   TNA. WO166/6018.

19.   TNA. MAF47/54.

20.   More, Bob and Kedorovitch, Kent (Editors). *The British Empire and the Italian Prisoner of War, 1940–1947.* Studies in Military & Strategic Histories Series.

21.   Bacque, James. *Other Losses.* Canada, 1989. (Information extracted from *The Times*, 2 October 1989.)

22.   Ministry of Labour and National Service Report, 1939–1946 (Cmd. 7225).

23.   Murray, K. A. H. *History of the Second World War: United Kingdom Civil Service.* Vol. 2, Agriculture, London, HMSO 1955.

24.   TNA. ADM1/10579.

25.   Brown, John. *The Un-melting Pot. An English Town and its Immigrants.* Macmillan & Co Ltd, 1970.

26.   TNA. CAB114/25.

27.   TNA. WO199/407.

28.   BLARS. Z1205/135.

29.   TNA. WO199/407.

30.   TNA. MAF47/54.

31.   TNA. MAF47/54. Return of votes from Bedfordshire hostels on change to Italian co-operator status on 15 September 1945:

Hostel	For co-operator status	Against co-operator status
Ravensden	143	12
Milton Ernest	29	113
Highlands	78	1
Ampthill	3	58
Harold	37	9
Total	290	193

32. TNA. WO199/409.
33. TNA. WO293 series.
34. TNA. FO916/581. Translated by John Sainsbury, December 2006.
35. TNA. MAF47/54.
36. In August 1943, the Camp Liaison Officer for Bedfordshire, Buckinghamshire, Huntingdonshire, Isle of Ely, Lincolnshire, Norfolk, Northamptonshire, Nottinghamshire, Rutland, Soke of Peterborough and Suffolk was Mr J. M. Dymond, c/o Divisional Road Engineers, Ministry of War Transport, Palace Chambers, Silver Street, Bedford.
37. TNA. MAF47/54.
38. TNA. WO32/9935.
39. TNA. WO166/6018.
40. BLARS. Z1205/197.
41. TNA. WO166/6018.
42. TNA. WO166/6018.
43. TNA. CO152/77.
44. TNA. WO166/6018.
45. TNA. WO166/6018.
46. BLARS BOR.B.CeS. Register of Service Burials.
47. BLARS CO/INQ1/4/N2. Reginald G. Rose, Coroner, recorded the following in his expenses ledger: Inquest 360. 15/07/43 Antonio Amedeo: Justifiable Homicide. Inquest 364. 30/08/43 Fillipo SAPIA: Suicide Inquest 510. 20/01/47 Alfred Ruf: Suicide. Inquest 539. 29/07/47 Bruno Shulz: Misadventure [Road traffic accident].
48. IRCC report dated 28/06/47 mentions this man dying of apoplexy. His place of burial is unknown.
49. TNA. WO166/6018.
50. TNA. MEPO2/6871.
51. TNA. MEPO2/6871.
52. Home Office Circular 227/44.
53. 'The Front Line of Freedom: British Farming in the Second World War.' Eds. Brian Short, Charles Watkins and John Martin. *The Agricultural History Review Supplement*, Series 4. British Agricultural History Society. Exeter, 2006.
54. TNA. FO916/308.
55. Ramsden, John. *Don't Mention The War*. London, 2006.
56. TNA. FO939/110.
57. Association of Jewish Refugees. April 2007 Journal.
58. Kendal Burt & James Leasor. Random House, *The One That Got Away*, New York, 1956.

59. Suffolk Record Office, Ipswich. HD 451/1. Von Werra made his first unsuccessful escape on 7 October 1940 from Satterwaite PoW Camp, near Alverston, Derbyshire.

60. Kochan, Miriam, *Prisoners of England*, The MacMillan Press Ltd, 1988.

61. TNA. WO32/14552.

62. TNA. WO166/14518.

63. BLARS. Z1205/060.

64. John Shelton was invested by HM King George VI at Buckingham Palace on 17 October 1944.

65. HMSO. Home Guard Information Circular, No. 41–15, xii, 1943 and by Sainsbury, J. D. *Hazardous Work*.

66. *Hunts Post*, 16 and 22 July 1943; *Bedford Record* 13 July; and *Bedfordshire Times*, 16 July 1943.

67. TNA. WO166/13927. The weather on 9 July 1943 was described as being dull and windy. For 10 July it was fair but cool.

68. TNA. MAF32. When searching for the farm I found the wartime British farm Survey to be an extremely useful source of information, providing details on 85 per cent of British farms. It has been referred to as the second Doomsday Book.

69. Interview with John Shelton.

70. *Weekend*, 21–27 May 1969.

71. More, Bob and Kedorovitch, Kent (Editors). *The British Empire and the Italian Prisoner of War, 1940–1947*. Studies in Military & Strategic Histories Series.

72. Private information from unpublished papers of the Whitbread family.

73. Gillman, Peter and Leni. *Collar the Lot. How Britain Interned and Expelled its Wartime Refugees*. Quartet Books Ltd, 1980.

74. BLARS. Z1205/143 and 1938 Kelly's Directory: Giancomo Zachtilla – General stores. The business survived the war as the 1949 and 1950 Kelly's Directories still listed the shop.

75. *Daily Mirror*, 27 April 1940.

76. Kushner, Tony. *We Europeans? Mass-Observation, 'Race' and British Identity in the Twentieth Century*. Aldershot, 2004, Ashgate.

77. Charmley, John. *Duff Cooper. The Authorised Biography*. Papermac, London, 1987.

78. Gillman, Peter and Leni. *Collar the Lot. How Britain Interned and Expelled its Wartime Refugees*. Quartet Books Ltd, 1980.

79. TNA. PREM 3/361/1.

80. 'Procedure for Employment of P. W. Without Guards', n.d., Series MP742/1, Item 255/21/51, Part V, pp.10-11, NAA Melbourne. Recorded in Italian PoW in NSW.

81. More Cooper, Richard. *Prisoners of War and the Struggle for Production, 1939–49.* 'The Front Line of Freedom: British Farming in the Second World War.' Eds. Brian Short, Charles Watkins and John Martin. *The Agricultural History Review Supplement*, Series 4. British Agricultural History Society. Exeter, 2006.

82. TNA. WO166/495.

83. Suffolk Record Office, Ipswich. HD 451/1.

84. HMSO. RAF pamphlet – 'The Stranger Within our Gates,' 1941.

85. HMSO. Anonymous PR Officer. *They Sought Out Rommel.* London, 1941.

86. Kushner, Tony. *We Europeans? Mass-Observation, 'Race' and British Identity in the Twentieth Century.* Aldershot, 2004, Ashgate.

87. Taylor, Philip M. (Ed.) *Britain and the Cinema in the Second World War*, MacMillan, Basingstoke, 1988.

88. Donald, Ralph R., *Savages, Swine and Buffoons.*

89. *The Times*, 10 August 1943.

90. TNA. CAB114/25.

91. Hansen, Eric G. *THE ITALIAN MILITARY ENIGMA.* Paper presented to USMC Command and Staff College Education Center, Marine Corps Combat Development Command Quantico, Virginia 22134, 2 May 1988.

92. *The Times* Online, 25 May 2001.

93. Percival, Winifred. *Not Only Music, Signora.* Sherratt, Altrincham, 1947.

94. BLARS. Z1205/141. Male farmer's son born on 21 October 1923.

95. BLARS. Z1205/109. Irish labourer in brickfields.

96. BLARS. Z1205/056. Male farmer's son.

97. *The Times*, 26 July 1943.

98. TNA. WO166/6018.

99. These rings are still talked of in village communities as being frequent gifts, but it has been impossible to locate anyone who still possesses one. The lack of surviving Italian PoW made artifacts, against other wartime items, suggests gifts or sales may not have been widespread or valued. German made toys appear to be more common.

100. TNA. FO939/357.

101. BLARS. Z1205/023.

102. Information from Mrs Thelma Marks, Colmworth and Neighbours History Society.

103. More, Bob and Kedorovitch, Kent (Editors). *The British Empire and the Italian Prisoner of War, 1940–1947.* Studies in Military & Strategic Histories Series.

104. Private information from German ex-PoW.

105. More, Bob and Kedorovitch, Kent (Editors). *The British Empire and the Italian Prisoner of War, 1940–1947.* Studies in Military & Strategic Histories Series.

106. TNA. MAF47/54.

107. TNA. FO916/581. Translated by John Sainsbury, December 2006.

108. BLARS. Z1205/027.

109. BLARS. Z1205/141.

110. TNA. WO166/6018.

111. *News Chronicle*, 27 April 1944.

112. TNA. WO166/6071.

113. TNA. WO166/6018.

114. TNA. MAF47/54.

115. *The Times*, 20 April 1944.

116. *Farmers Weekly*, 10 January 1941.

117. *Daily Express*, 9 January 1942.

118. *Farmers Weekly*, 15 December 1942.

119. *Farmers Weekly*, 20 February 1943.

120. PD Commons 409, 20 March 1945.

121. Brown, John. *The Un-melting Pot. An English Town and its Immigrants.* Macmillan & Co Ltd, 1970.

122. Brown, John. *The Un-melting Pot. An English Town and its Immigrants.* Macmillan & Co Ltd, 1970.

123. TNA. FO898/325.

124. Manning, John, *The Bedfordshire Magazine*, Vol. XXV, pp. 231-236.

125. Ramsden, John. *Don't Mention The War.* London, 2006.

126. Ramsden, John. *Don't Mention The War.* London, 2006.

127. Ramsden, John. *Don't Mention The War.* London, 2006.

128. Vansittart, Sir Robert. *Black Record: Germans Past and Present.* London, 1941.

129. Zeigler, Philip. *London at War 1939–1945.* London, 1995.

130. Sulivan, Matthew Barry. *Thresholds of Peace. German Prisoners and the People of Britain 1944–48.* Hamish Hamilton, London.

131. Montgomery, Bernard Law, *Viscount Montgomery of Alamein*, London, 1958.

132. BLARS. Z1205/060.

133. BLARS. Z1205/043.

134. BLARS. Z1205/122.

135. Sulivan, Matthew Barry. *Thresholds of Peace. German Prisoners and the People of Britain 1944–48.* Hamish Hamilton, London.

136. BLARS. Z1205/171.
137. BLARS. Z1205/016.
138. Antrobus, Stuart. *We wouldn't have missed it for the world. The Women's Land Army in Bedfordshire 1939–1950.* Copt Hewick, North Yorkshire, 2008.
139. TNA. FO939/140.
140. BLARS. X819/9/6.
141. BLARS. Z1205/154.
142. TNA. MAF47/54.
143. Denne Parker, Henry Michael, *History of the Second World War: United Kingdom Civil Service.* Vol. 5; *ManPoWer: A Study of War-Time Policy and Administration.* London HMSO, 1957.
144. TNA. FO916/1275.
145. TNA. FO916/581. Translated by John Sainsbury, December 2006.
146. *Daily Express*, 9 January 1942.
147. BLARS. Z1205/109.
148. BLARS. Z1205/060.
149. *The Times*, 14 May 1945.
150. TNA. CAB114/25.
151. TNA. WO199/407.
152. TNA. MEPO2/6871.
153. TNA. MEPO2/6871.
154. Taylor, Pamela Howe. *Enemies Become Friends.*
155. BLARS. Z1205/109.
156. Ramsden, John. *Don't Mention The War.* London, 2006.
157. More Cooper, Richard. *Prisoners of War and the Struggle for Production, 1939–49.* 'The Front Line of Freedom: British Farming in the Second World War.' Eds. Brian Short, Charles Watkins and John Martin. *The Agricultural History Review Supplement*, Series 4. British Agricultural History Society. Exeter, 2006.
158. Taylor, Philip M. (Ed.) *Britain and the Cinema in the Second World War*, MacMillan, Basingstoke, 1988.
159. Hall, John, *Private Memories, Public Perceptions: Italian Prisoners of War in Northern New South Wales.* LIMINA Vol. 5, 1999
160. Summerfield, Penny and Corinna Peniston-Bird. *Contesting Home Defence. Men, Women and the Home Guard in the Second World War.*
161. http://www.bbc.co.uk/ww2peopleswar
162. BBC 'People's War'. Claude H. C. Banks.
163. *Daily Mail*, 2 June 1998.
164. Baker, Arthur. *A Taste of Freedom; Stories of the German and Italian Prisoners who Escaped from Camps in Britain during World War II.* Robert Jackson. London, 1964.

165.   The book contains no references. I have been unable to contact the author to establish his sources.

166.   More, Bob and Kedorovitch, Kent (Editors). *The British Empire and the Italian Prisoner of War, 1940–1947.* Studies in Military & Strategic Histories Series.

167.   TNA. WO24/957.

168.   TNA. HO215/201.

169.   TNA. FO939/152.

170.   TNA. FO939/152.

171.   TNA. FO939/152.

Bibliography

ARCHIVE RESOURCES

TNA. 25/11/41.

TNA. ADM1/10579.

TNA. ADM1/11640.

TNA. CAB114/25. Employment of Italian PoW in agriculture, 1941–42.

TNA. CO 152/77. Colonial Office. Re-education of German PoW, 1946.

TNA. CO 875/11/12.

TNA. FO898/325. Treatment and status of Italian prisoners: Correspondence and reports.

TNA. FO916/308.

TNA. FO916/581. PoW camps in the United Kingdom – ICRC reports 1943.

TNA. FO916/1275. Italian prisoners of war – treatment 1945.

TNA. FO939/110.

TNA. FO939/140.

TNA. FO939/152. 72 Working Camp, Ducks Cross Camp, Colmworth, Bedfordshire

TNA. FO939/357. Policy towards Italian PoW after surrender of Italy 1943–44.

TNA. HO215/201. PoW camps in the UK: list of locations and copies of administrative instructions.

TNA. MAF 32. National Farm Survey of England and Wales, 1940–43.

TNA. MAF47/54. PoW: employment on agricultural work; general policy, 1939–45.

TNA. MEPO 2/6871. Scheme for German/Italian PoW brought into the UK as agricultural workers.

TNA. PREM 3/361/1. Prime Minister's Office: Operational Correspondence and Papers.

TNA. WO24/957. War Establishments 1945 July-December.

TNA. WO32/9904.

TNA. WO32/9935.

TNA. WO32/14552.

TNA. WO166/495.

TNA. WO166/6018. Home Forces: War Diaries, Second World War. Eastern Command. 1942 Jan. – Dec.

TNA. WO166/6071. Home Forces: War Diaries, Second World War. 2 Corps G Branch. 1942 Jan. – Dec.

TNA. WO166/10931. Home Forces: War Diaries, Second World War. Beds & Hunts Sub District.

TNA. WO166/13927.

TNA. WO166/13997. Home Forces: War Diary, Second World War. 297 Coy, Pioneer Corps.

TNA. WO166/14518.

TNA. WO199/407. GHQ. PoW Employment and accommodation 1942–44.

TNA. WO293 series. Army Council Instructions, containing instructions on treatment of PoW.

BLARS. BOR B.Ce5. Register of Service Burials for Bedford Cemetery.

BLARS CO/INQ1/4/N2.

BLARS. X 819/9/6. Transcript of interview of Tom Skeffington – Lodge by Len Holden.

BLARS. Z50/29/13. Bedfordshire Times Collection.

BLARS. Z50/29/14. Bedfordshire Times Collection.

BLARS. Z1205/016. Transcript of interview: Male brickworker.

BLARS. Z1205/023. Transcript of interview: Giuseppina Schiavone.

BLARS. Z1205/027. Transcript of interview: Female farming family member.

BLARS. Z1205/043. Transcript of interview: Female brickworker

BLARS. Z1205/056. Transcript of interview: Male farmer's son.

BLARS. Z1205/060. Transcript of interview: Male brickworker.

BLARS. Z1205/109. Transcript of interview: Irish labourer in brickfields.

BLARS. Z1205/122. Transcript of interview.

BLARS. Z1205/135.

BLARS. Z1205/141. Transcript of interview: Male farmer's son born 21/10/23.

BLARS. Z1205/143 Transcript of interview.

BLARS. Z1205/154. Transcript of interview: unidentified WLA girl.

BLARS. Z1205/171. Transcript of interview.

BLARS. Verbal information from unpublished papers of the Whitbread family.

BLARS. The Bedfordshire Magazine Vol. XXV. pp. 231–236. Manning, John. Rebuilding Highlands Farm.
Suffolk Record Office, Ipswich. HD 451/1. Numerous Home Guard bulletins.

BRITISH LIBRARY NEWSPAPER READING ROOM

Bedford Record, 13 July.
Bedfordshire Times, 16 July 1943.
Daily Express, 9 January 1942.
Daily Mail, 2 June 1998.
Daily Mirror, 27 April 1940.
Farmers Weekly, 10 January 1941.
Farmers Weekly, 28 February 1941.
Farmers Weekly, 15 December 1942.
Farmers Weekly, 20 February 1943.
Hunts Post, 15 and 22 July 1943.
News Chronicle, 27 April 1944.
The Times, 26 July 1943.
The Times, 10 August 1943.
The Times, 20 April 1944.
The Times, 14 May 1945.
Weekend, May 21–27 1969.

NON-ARCHIVE SOURCES

Interview with John Shelton.
Conversations with Eddi Petri and Hans Pueschel (ex-German PoW).
Telephone conversation with Mrs Thelma Marks, Colmworth and Neighbours History Society.

PRINTED SOURCES (PUBLISHED)

Antrobus, Stuart. *We wouldn't have missed it for the world. The Women's Land Army in Bedfordshire 1939–1950*. Copt Hewick, North Yorkshire, 2008.
Association of Jewish Refugees. April 2007 Journal.
Baker, Arthur. *A Taste of Freedom; Stories of the German and Italian Prisoners who Escaped from Camps in Britain during World War II.*

Robert Jackson. London, 1964.

Bacque, James. *Other Losses*. Canada, 1989. (Information extracted from *The Times*, 2 October 1989.)

Berretta, A. *Prigineri di Churchill*. Milan, 1951.

Brown, John. *The Un-melting Pot. An English Town and its Immigrants*. Macmillan & Co Ltd, 1970.

Calder, Angus. *The People's War*. Jonathan Cape, London, 1969.

Charmley, John. *Duff Cooper. The Authorised Biography*. Papermac, London, 1987.

Conti Flavio Giovanni. *I prigioneri di Guerra Italian*. Bologna, 1986.

Costello, John. *Love, Sex & War*. London, Collins, 1985.

Denne Parker, Henry Michael, *History of the Second World War: United Kingdom Civil Service*. Vol. 5; *ManPoWer: A Study of War-Time Policy and Administration*. London HMSO, 1957.

Duberly, Col. *A Short History of the 3rd Hunts Battalion, Home Guard*. 1940–44, Privately published.

Eley, Geoff. *Finding the People's War: Film, British Collective Memory, and World War II. The American Historical Review*, Vol. 106, No. 3, (Jun., 2001).

Field, Geoffrey, 'Social Patriotism and the British Working Class Appearance and Disappearance of a Tradition.' *International Labor and Working Class History* 42 (Fall 1992): 27. Quoted in Geoff Eley, 'Finding the People's War: Film, British Collective Memory, and World War II,' *The American Historical Review*, Vol. 106, No. 3. (Jun., 2001), pp. 818–838.

Gillman, Peter and Leni. *Collar the Lot. How Britain Interned and Expelled its Wartime Refugees*. Quartet Books Ltd, 1980.

Hansard, House of Commons, fifth series (1939–40).

HMSO. Anonymous PR Officer. *They Sought Out Rommel*. London, 1941.

HMSO. Home Guard Information Circular, No. 41–15, xii, 1943 and by Sainsbury, J. D. *Hazardous Work*.

HMSO. RAF pamphlet – 'The Stranger within our gates', 1941.

Home Office Circular 227/44.

Kelly's Directory for Bedfordshire, 1938.

Kochan, Miriam, *Prisoners of England*, The MacMillan Press Ltd, 1988.

Kushner, Tony. *We Europeans? Mass-Observation, 'Race' and British Identity in the Twentieth Century*. Aldershot, 2004, Ashgate.

Lafitte, Francois. *The Internment of Aliens*. Penquin, 1940 (re-printed Libris, 1980).

Ministry of Labour and National Service Report, 1939–1946 (Cmd. 7225)

Molony, G. J. C. *History of the Second World War. The Mediterranean and Middle East*, HMSO, 1973.

Montgomery, J. K. 'The Maintenance of the Agricultural Labour Supply in England & Wales during the War.' *International Review of Agriculture*, Rome, 1922. (Originally published in the *International Review of Agricultural Economics*.) Reviewed *The Economic Journal*, Vol. 33, No. 130 (June 1923), pp 232–234.

Montgomery, Bernard Law, *Viscount Montgomery of Alamein*, London, 1958.

More Bob and Kedorovitch, Kent (Eds). *Prisoners of War and their Captors in World War 2*. Berg Publishers, Oxford, 1996.

More, Bob and Kedorovitch, Kent (Editors). *The British Empire and the Italian Prisoner of War, 1940–1947*. Studies in Military & Strategic Histories Series.

Moore, Bob and Hately-Broad, Barbara (Editors). *Prisoners of War, Prisoners of Peace*. Berg, 2005.

More Cooper, Richard. *Prisoners of War and the Struggle for Production, 1939–49*. 'The Front Line of Freedom: British Farming in the Second World War.' Eds. Brian Short, Charles Watkins and John Martin. *The Agricultural History Review Supplement*, Series 4. British Agricultural History Society. Exeter, 2006.

Murray, K. A. H. *History of the Second World War: United Kingdom Civil Service*. Vol. 2, Agriculture, London, HMSO 1955.

Percival, Winifred. *Not Only Music, Signora*. Sherratt, Altrincham, 1947.

'Procedure for Employment of P. W. Without Guards', n.d., Series MP742/1, Item 255/21/51, Part V, pp.10-11, NAA Melbourne. Recorded in Italian PoW in NSW.

Rainaro Romain H. (Ed.) *I prigioneri militari durante la seconda guerre mondiale: espetti e problemi storei*. Milan, 1985.

Ramsden, John. *Don't Mention The War*. London, 2006.

Rose, Sonya O. *Which People's War? National Identity and Citizenship in Britain 1939–45*. Oxford University Press, 2003.

Sainsbury, J. D. *Hazardous Work*. Hart Books, Welwyn, 1985.

Stent, Ronald. *'A Bespattered Page'. The Internment of His Majesty's Most Loyal Enemy Aliens*. Andre Deutsch.

Sulivan, Matthew Barry. *Thresholds of Peace. German Prisoners and the People of Britain 1944–48*. Hamish Hamilton, London.

Summerfield, Penny and Corinna Peniston-Bird. *Contesting Home Defence. Men, Women and the Home Guard in the Second World War*.

Taylor, Pamela Howe. *Enemies Become Friends*.

Taylor, Philip M. (Ed.) *Britain and the Cinema in the Second World War*, MacMillan, Basingstoke, 1988.

Vansittart, Sir Robert. *Black Record: Germans Past and Present*. London, 1941.

Zeigler, Philip. *London at War 1939–1945*. London, 1995.

PRINTED SOURCES (UNPUBLISHED)

Donald, Ralph R. *Savages, Swine and Buffoons.*   http://www.imagesjournal.com/issue08/features/wwii/article.htm.

Hall, John, *Private Memories, Public Perceptions: Italian Prisoners of War in Northern New South Wales*. LIMINA Vol. 5, 1999

Hansen, Eric G. *THE ITALIAN MILITARY ENIGMA*. Paper presented to USMC Command and Staff College Education Center, Marine Corps Combat Development Command Quantico, Virginia 22134, 2 May 1988.